The Unconscious Motives of Romantic Attraction

The Reasons behind Recurring Unhealthy Relationship Patterns

Renaldy Fabien, EdD

ISBN: 9781696294386

Preface

Romantic attraction has captivated human hearts and minds for centuries. Countless thinkers have attempted to unravel the mysteries behind why men and women are drawn to one another, offering theories that aim to make sense of this deeply emotional and complex experience. Over time, our understanding of love has evolved, revealing not only insights but also inconsistencies and contradictions across different schools of thought.

One of the challenges in exploring this topic lies in the nature of academic inquiry itself: researchers often interpret romantic attraction through the lens of the specific truths they uncover. While these individual perspectives offer valuable insights, they don't always align. Yet, it is precisely through the interplay of diverse viewpoints that a richer understanding can emerge. Rather than subscribing to a single, definitive theory, this book embraces a multidisciplinary approach, recognizing that the phenomenon of love is too nuanced to be confined to one framework.

In developing the ideas presented in this book, several influential theories were considered. Key among them are Sigmund Freud's concepts of *anaclitic* and *narcissistic* object choices, as well as the ethological notion of *sexual imprinting*, which suggests that early relational experiences shape our adult preferences. Love, in this context, becomes a reactivation of early childhood emotional states and relational patterns — a revisiting of the tender bonds formed during infancy.

A compelling argument for understanding adult romantic attachment is rooted in exploring the emotional imprints left by early life experiences. The foundation for love is established through our formative interactions with caregivers and our immediate environment. While proximity and current circumstances can influence attraction, the origins of love often reach far deeper, rooted in the affective residue of our earliest relationships.

Unlike many relationship guides that offer prescriptive advice or one-size-fits-all solutions, this book is not intended as a manual filled with fixed answers. Instead, it serves as a diagnostic tool — an invitation for readers to explore and understand their own relational patterns. The aim is to illuminate the underlying motivations that shape romantic choices, thereby enabling individuals to make more conscious and fulfilling decisions in their love lives.

At its core, this book rests on the belief that meaningful change in our romantic lives begins with self-awareness. Without a clear understanding of who we are and what drives us, it becomes difficult — if not impossible — to build a healthy and harmonious relationship with another person. By examining the emotional forces that influence our attractions, we take the first step toward more intentional, resilient, and authentic love.

Acknowledgment

This book began as a personal journey to uncover the deeper truth behind what drives romantic attraction. Years of informal observation, paired with an extensive review of the literature on love and relationships, led to a central realization: the emotion we call love often stems from unconscious motivations. When someone is in love, it is rarely easy — if ever — to rationally explain why they are drawn to a particular person.

Seventeenth-century French philosopher Blaise Pascal famously said, "The heart has its reasons, which reason knows nothing about." This book does not aim to provide conventional advice on how to find or keep a partner. Rather, it explores a more fundamental question: *Why*, out of countless possible choices, are we drawn to one person over others? In seeking that answer, we gain valuable insight into the recurring patterns — both constructive and destructive — that define our romantic lives.

In today's world, where online dating has become a mainstream avenue for connection, it has never been easier for singles to meet potential partners. Dating platforms enable individuals to present curated versions of themselves and to seek others who align with their stated values and long-term goals. Yet, even in the digital age, the choices we make in love reflect more than just logic or compatibility. They mirror our innermost emotional landscape — often shaped by unconscious desires and unresolved internal conflicts.

Understanding these hidden influences can be transformative. No matter how many options modern technology offers, we are likely to be drawn to someone whose personality resonates with our own unconscious patterns. Virtual dating may expand access to potential partners, but it does not exempt us from the emotional scripts we unknowingly follow.

This book is intended as a relationship enrichment resource for both singles and married individuals. For couples, it serves as a guide to self-awareness and emotional growth, offering insights that can support the health and longevity of a committed partnership. For single individuals, it provides foundational understanding that can inform future relationship choices and lay the groundwork for a fulfilling and lasting bond.

Table of Contents

Page

Chapter 1: Introduction.................................1

Chapter 2: The Concept of Romantic Attraction...........8

Chapter 3: The Origin and the Exact Nature of Love...19

    Love and the Ancient Greek Philosophy.............20

    The Anaclitic Object Choice 25

    The Narcissistic Object Choice...................28

    The Construct of anima and Animus................31

    The Imprinting Phenomenon........................35

    Physical Attractiveness 41

Chapter 4: The Pathological Aspect of Love..............46

    The Cinderello Complex...........................58

    Why Date a Cinderello? 61

    The Cinderella Complex 63

Chapter 5: A Quest toward Complementarity 67

    Psychological and Evolutionary Perspectives.....68

    Interpersonal Theory of Personality 73

    The Rediscovery of Self 78

Chapter 6: The Narcissistic Love Object Choice 88

    Self-Erasing Strategies 98

The Entitled Lover 101

Chapter 7: Parental Image and Romantic Choice 105

Positive Sexual Imprinting.... 110

Negative Sexual Imprinting...........................116

Chapter 8: Human Sexuality...........................122

The Multidisciplinary Approach of Human Sexuality.....................................124

Love Making...........................126

Chapter 9: Conclusion 131

Chapter 10: References 136

Introduction

The feeling that draws you toward a relationship with someone of the opposite sex is commonly referred to as romantic or sexual attraction. Today, this powerful emotional experience is often labeled as *love* — a deep desire directed toward someone who captivates your heart, someone you admire intensely and feel joyfully drawn to. When in love, that person becomes the center of your attention and affection.

You may find yourself constantly thinking about this "special someone," asking, *Why him? Why her?* Although you might attempt to explain your feelings, deep down, you sense that your attraction defies logic. Love often escapes the boundaries of rational understanding — it soars beyond the limits of conscious reasoning.

Love is a profound and multifaceted emotion that has fascinated humanity for centuries. From ancient poetry to modern films, love has inspired countless expressions of longing and devotion. Romantic attraction — a key dimension of love — is a complex interplay of biology, psychology, and sociology. To fully grasp this phenomenon, we must explore its many layers: from the biochemical impulses that ignite passion to the cultural norms that shape our ideas about love (Fisher, 2004).

Often described as "chemistry," love is fueled by internal forces that draw us toward another person. Like hunger or thirst, love is believed to be a biologically based drive. When we feel attracted to someone, the brain releases a cascade of chemicals — including dopamine, norepinephrine, and serotonin — which produce the intense euphoria of new love (Young & Wang, 2004). These neurotransmitters energize us, suppress appetite, and narrow our focus onto the beloved.

Dopamine, commonly known as the "feel-good" neurotransmitter, activates the brain's pleasure and reward systems, contributing to the sense of joy and motivation experienced in romantic connection (Aron et al., 2005). Norepinephrine, closely linked to adrenaline, accounts for physical symptoms like a racing heart, sweaty palms, and heightened excitement (Marazziti et al., 1999). Meanwhile, serotonin levels often decrease during early stages of love, potentially explaining the obsessive thoughts that accompany new relationships.

Another important factor is pheromones — subtle chemical signals that influence human attraction through scent and subconscious recognition (Grammer et al., 2005). While their role in human behavior is not as pronounced as in other animals, studies suggest they may still contribute to the magnetic pull between individuals.

This initial magnetic force is often referred to as the "spark" — a unique, intangible connection felt when two people resonate on multiple levels: emotional, physical, intellectual, spiritual, and even ideological. Culturally, we reference this spark in music and conversation: "I didn't feel a spark when I kissed him." But this spark isn't just a poetic metaphor — it often correlates with genuine emotional and physiological responses driven by mutual compatibility.

Psychological research, including the work of Helen Fisher, suggests the spark results from a surge of dopamine and norepinephrine, heightening our perception and excitement in the presence of a potential partner (Fisher, 2004). A 2012 study by Eastwick, Finkel, and Eagly revealed that we're most likely to feel a spark with individuals whose traits align with our personal ideals, values, or emotional needs.

While the spark can initiate a relationship, sustaining it requires emotional maturity, communication, and commitment. The early thrill may fade, but lasting love is built on deeper bonds. A spark may signal chemistry, but not compatibility.

To illustrate, consider the metaphor of electricity. A spark is generated when a strong positive charge connects with a strong negative charge — an energy surge that leaps across a gap. In relationships, this represents the intense pull between two individuals. We often recognize when a relationship is charged with passion — and when it isn't. The presence of a spark can bring joy and connection; its absence often signals indifference or emotional distance.

In the early stages of love, the spark brings exhilaration. Time spent together is never dull, and even ordinary moments feel magical. Conversely, the absence of this spark reveals itself in emotional detachment, apathy, and a lack of affectionate gestures.

However, it's crucial to distinguish between *passionate love* and *lust*. These two experiences, though similar in intensity, are fundamentally different. Lust is rooted in sexual desire and immediate gratification, while passionate love involves a deeper emotional bond and a longing for intimacy and connection. Passionate love is enriched by mutual vulnerability, shared dreams, and a commitment to growth. It's not just about physical attraction; it integrates emotional, intellectual, and spiritual dimensions.

Lust, in contrast, is more superficial and transient. It often disregards emotional depth and long-term connection, focusing instead on physical pleasure. Lust can lead individuals to objectify others, ignoring the importance of empathy, care, or moral boundaries. In extreme cases, lust drives people to pursue forbidden or destructive relationships — illustrating its irrational and antisocial potential. In contrast, passionate love builds a foundation for healthy, lasting relationships.

The challenge of understanding what drives romantic attraction is one of humanity's oldest questions. From ancient philosophers like Plato to modern psychoanalysts, anthropologists, sociologists, and psychologists, scholars have long attempted to unravel the mysteries of romantic desire.

Each discipline offers valuable insights. A psychoanalyst may explore unconscious motivations influencing partner choice, while a sociologist might focus on external factors such as culture, religion, ethnicity, or social class. These perspectives are not contradictory — they are complementary. While external factors offer a range of possibilities, our psychological blueprint determines which option we ultimately choose.

Romantic attraction is often rooted in unconscious factors, including patterns formed early in life. These may involve positive or negative imprinting or a desire to reconnect with an idealized version of oneself. As this book will explore, our romantic choices are rarely random — they often reflect deeply ingrained emotional patterns.

By the end of this book, you'll gain a clearer understanding of why we're drawn to certain people and why, despite our best intentions, we sometimes repeat the same mistakes in love. This exploration invites you to look inward, recognize your own relational patterns, and, most importantly, take the first steps toward more meaningful and fulfilling romantic connections.

The Concept of Romantic Attraction

Romantic attraction is an emotional and psychological inclination toward forming a close, intimate bond with another person. It often involves feelings of love, a desire for companionship, and deep emotional connection. While romantic and sexual attraction frequently coexist, they are distinct experiences; romantic attraction emphasizes emotional closeness and affection, whereas sexual attraction centers on physical desire.

A range of factors influence romantic attraction, including biological, psychological, social, and cultural elements. According to Diamond (2003), it emerges from a complex interplay between neurobiological mechanisms and social conditioning, guiding individuals toward forming affectionate, committed relationships. Sternberg's Triangular Theory of Love (1986) offers further insight, identifying three essential components — intimacy, passion, and commitment — which combine in various ways to produce different types of love.

Cultural context also shapes how romantic attraction is understood and expressed. For instance,

Hendrick and Hendrick (1992) identified various love styles, such as *Eros* (passionate love) and *Pragma* (practical love), underscoring the diversity of romantic expression across individuals and societies.

In certain European cultures, such as France, the concept of *sexual attraction* is often used to describe the emotional and physical connection one feels toward someone of the opposite sex. In contrast, American culture tends to favor the term *romantic attraction*, which carries a more emotionally nuanced and socially acceptable connotation. Discussions in the United States typically emphasize romantic attraction and romantic choice over sexual attraction, perhaps reflecting broader cultural attitudes toward intimacy and propriety.

Nonetheless, romantic and sexual attraction frequently overlap. Both involve emotional intensity and the desire for connection, whether expressed physically, emotionally, or both. For the purposes of this book, the term *romantic attraction* will be used more frequently to reflect the broader emotional scope of love and connection.

Romantic attraction is a rich and multifaceted concept that plays a central role in human relationships and social dynamics. It typically involves a profound emotional connection, accompanied by feelings of passion, intimacy, and commitment. At its core, romantic attraction is characterized by a strong emotional bond between individuals, often expressed through affection, empathy, and warmth. This emotional connection fosters trust, understanding, and a sense of closeness, forming the bedrock of most romantic relationships.

While emotional intimacy is essential, physical attraction also plays a significant role. This includes an interest in another person's physical appearance, body language, or presence. Physical attraction can be shaped by a variety of influences—ranging from biological instincts and evolutionary cues to cultural norms and personal preferences.

Two key elements that often accompany romantic attraction are intimacy and passion. Intimacy involves the willingness to share personal thoughts, feelings, and experiences, deepening the emotional connection.

Passion, on the other hand, refers to the intense emotions and desire often felt in romantic relationships, marked by excitement and longing to be close to the beloved.

In many cases, emotional rapport between a man and a woman carries an underlying sexual dimension. This is not to suggest that every emotional connection between individuals of the opposite sex is explicitly sexual, but rather that romantic love often includes a physical component. Sexual desire may not be the only reason people connect, but it is frequently a motivating force in romantic relationships. Though love involves far more than physical intimacy, sex has a unique power to deepen emotional bonding and add a layer of intensity that few other experiences can match.

This dynamic is reflected in the language we use. For instance, the term "making love" is often used to describe sexual intercourse not only as a physical act but as an expression of deep emotional connection. While acts like kissing, touching, and cuddling may not always lead to intercourse, they are often viewed as expressions of romantic or sexual interest. In that sense, a relationship that includes physical affection or the potential for sexual intimacy can be described as *sexual*, not solely in reference to intercourse, but in acknowledgment of the emotional and physical chemistry between two people.

Ultimately, romantic attraction blends emotional and physical elements, creating a powerful force that draws people together and shapes how they form and sustain relationships.

Many people find it difficult to imagine a relationship between a man and a woman that is based solely on sex or physical intimacy. No matter how enjoyable the sexual experience may be, such a relationship is unlikely to endure beyond a few weeks or months. While it's true that a healthy sexual connection can enhance a romantic relationship, it is also widely accepted that sex alone cannot sustain a meaningful or lasting bond.

When the foundation of a relationship is purely physical, emotional disconnection often follows. After the initial excitement fades and physical needs are satisfied, there is often little desire to remain in that person's company. Over time, what we truly long for is someone who resonates with our inner self—someone with whom we can share not only physical closeness but also emotional intimacy, shared values, and meaningful conversation. As the Bible puts it, we seek "a mate fit for us." Without that deeper compatibility, long-term commitment becomes unsatisfying, regardless of physical chemistry. While sexual attraction may initiate a connection, emotional comfort is what sustains it.

In recent years, a new trend has emerged in modern dating culture—what is often referred to as a "friends with benefits" or "no strings attached" relationship. A growing number of single individuals are turning to these arrangements for various reasons. Many cite a lack of time for serious relationships, prioritizing career or personal freedom over romantic commitment. Others believe that keeping their options open with multiple partners increases their chances of eventually finding the right one.

One need only browse an online dating platform to see how common this mindset has become. A typical profile might read: "Hi, I'm Linda. I'm focused on my career right now and don't have time for a serious relationship. I'm just looking for someone to hang out with occasionally—no pressure. If you're interested, drop me a line with your picture and a little about yourself." While such messages may appear straightforward, they also raise important questions. Is Linda truly constrained by time, or is there something deeper—perhaps an emotional hesitation or unresolved psychological issue—that underlies her reluctance to pursue meaningful connection?

Ultimately, while casual arrangements may serve a temporary purpose for some, they rarely provide the depth, security, and fulfillment that come from a committed romantic relationship built on mutual respect, understanding, and emotional compatibility. Human beings are inherently wired to love and be loved. No matter how much we accomplish in life—career success, wealth, recognition—without meaningful love, we often feel as though something essential is missing. Heartbreak, unreciprocated love, or emotional detachment can take a profound toll on our mental, emotional, and even physical well-being (Fisher et al., 2010). If you asked a self-proclaimed "confirmed bachelor" or a "strong, independent woman" to speak candidly, many would admit to feeling an underlying sense of incompleteness despite their achievements.

From a young age, we are taught that humans are social creatures. Beyond biological needs, our well-being is deeply connected to our social environment. Among the most powerful social stimuli is companionship—especially romantic companionship. It brings a sense of wholeness and belonging: wholeness because having someone who understands and supports us fills an emotional void, and belonging because love affirms our place in the social world, making us feel connected rather than isolated.

No one truly wants to be alone. Everyone is searching—sometimes for someone specific, sometimes for something meaningful in another person. If being single were as fulfilling as it's often portrayed, far fewer people would seek out partners. Despite knowing the risks—like high divorce rates—many still choose to pursue love. Why? Because the desire to build a lasting, intimate bond outweighs the fear of failure. People long for more than just momentary pleasure; they crave emotional safety, shared experiences, and companionship that endures.

After all, isn't loneliness one of the greatest burdens of modern life—rivaled only by natural disasters and chronic illness in its emotional weight? We instinctively know that what money cannot buy is what matters most. Wealth may purchase temporary pleasures and superficial relationships, but it cannot create authentic love. Love, with its depth, vulnerability, and emotional connection, remains one of the few truly priceless experiences.

Sexual attraction often intertwines with romance, as romance encompasses actions and emotions driven by love and affection. It is more than just a feeling—it's a rich, multifaceted experience rooted in emotional intimacy, physical connection, and the desire to express care and affection toward a partner.

At its heart, romance is about cultivating a deep emotional bond. This bond is built on mutual trust, respect, and understanding. Through this connection, individuals feel safe to share their inner thoughts and vulnerabilities, creating a sense of closeness that goes beyond the physical. Passion and affection often accompany romance—whether it's holding hands, embracing, or simply spending quiet moments together. These physical expressions serve to strengthen the emotional connection and foster feelings of warmth and comfort.

Romance also thrives through thoughtful gestures and everyday acts of kindness. From writing love notes and planning surprise dates to simply being emotionally present, these actions show care and intention. They signal that the relationship is valued and nurtured, deepening the bond between partners.

Throughout history, romance has been a timeless theme in literature, art, music, and film. From the pages of *Pride and Prejudice* to Klimt's evocative painting *The Kiss*, romance has inspired creative works that capture the beauty and complexity of human emotion. Love songs and romantic films continue this tradition, portraying the ups and downs of relationships in ways that resonate with audiences around the world. These mediums allow people to vicariously experience and reflect on love's emotional depth.

Romance is also celebrated through meaningful occasions—anniversaries, weddings, and Valentine's Day—each offering moments to express appreciation and deepen emotional ties. In popular culture, romance is often visualized through iconic imagery: couples walking hand-in-hand, laughing together on a beach, or dressed in white running through waves. These depictions, while symbolic, reflect real-world romantic gestures like sending flowers, preparing a candlelit dinner, or writing a heartfelt song or poem.

In essence, romance is the expression of love through emotion, action, and connection. Whether grand or subtle, romantic gestures enrich relationships and help transform affection into enduring emotional bonds.

The Origin and the Exact Nature of Love

The quest for the other half of the self is a deeply rooted idea in philosophy, psychology, and literature, reflecting the human desire for completeness through love and connection. This concept suggests that individuals seek romantic partners not just for companionship but to fulfill a deeper, existential longing for wholeness.

A reflection on the motives underlying human sexual choice always tempts us to go back to Sigmund Freud. Sigmund Freud's contributions to the modern doctrine of amorous choice were deeply rooted in his psychoanalytic theories, particularly in relation to unconscious desires, childhood experiences, and psychological complexes. His work challenged traditional notions of love and attraction by emphasizing the hidden, often irrational forces that shape human relationships.

Freud argued that early childhood relationships, particularly with parents, play a crucial role in shaping later romantic preferences. Through the Oedipus complex, he suggested that individuals develop unconscious desires for the opposite-sex parent while experiencing rivalry with the same-sex parent (Freud, 1905/1953). These unconscious dynamics, he posited, later manifest in partner selection, as individuals often seek romantic partners who resemble their parental figures in some way (Freud, 1910/1957).

Love and Ancient Greek Philosophy

The exploration of love predates the theories of Freud and his contemporaries, reaching back to the era of ancient Greek philosophers. This intellectual journey is profoundly captured in Plato's work, "The Symposium." Here, Plato, alongside other philosophers such as Phaedrus, Pausanias, Eryximachus, Aristophanes, Agathon, Socrates, and Alcibiades, engages in a rich discussion about the true nature of love. "The Symposium," also known as "The Banquet," stands as a significant text in Western philosophy, offering a metaphysical exploration of love (Symposium, 189d–193d).

In "The Symposium," Plato introduces love, or *eros*, as a multifaceted and evolving concept. It surpasses mere physical attraction and leads individuals toward the pursuit of higher truth and wisdom. Through the speeches of various characters, the dialogue presents diverse perspectives on love, ultimately culminating in Socrates' account. Socrates introduces the concept of the Ladder of Love—a philosophical journey from physical desire to the appreciation of divine beauty.

To explain the origins of human sexual attraction, Aristophanes recounts a remarkable creation myth. In the beginning, humans had a very different nature. These original beings were androgynous, embodying both male and female characteristics. They possessed a single head with two faces, four arms, four legs, four eyes, four ears, and two sets of genitalia. Their immense strength led them to challenge the gods, prompting Zeus to split them in half as a way to weaken and discipline them. Afterward, Apollo tended to their wounds, and Zeus repositioned their genitalia to make sexual union possible when they embraced (*Symposium*, 189d–193d).

Plato's *Symposium* ultimately presents love as a transformative force that elevates the soul beyond mere physical desire, leading it toward intellectual and spiritual enlightenment. Love is not about possession or pleasure but about the pursuit of wisdom, virtue, and the eternal Form of Beauty.

Aristophanes' myth offers insight into the enduring question of why a person is drawn to one individual over another. The search for "the one" or a "perfect match" reflects a deeper yearning for completeness. At the core of every human being is a persistent longing to find the missing half of oneself—a soul mate—echoing what Levinas referred to as a "longing for the other."

You will not feel complete until you find the missing half of your soul. Aristophanes offers a metaphysical explanation for the nature of sexual and romantic attraction. His account provides a mystical perspective on why some people instinctively recognize what they are looking for in a partner.

Discovering the person who aligns with your essence can be seen as a rediscovery of your true self. In the presence of your other half, there is a natural sense of ease—no need to perform or pretend. Even if the impulse to impress arises, something in the other person's demeanor invites you to relax and be genuine.

What is the most telling sign of having made the right choice in love? Isn't it the feeling of peace you experience simply by being around that person? When love represents a reunion with the lost part of oneself, it brings calm rather than pressure.

The person who completes you is not someone trying to reshape you but someone who feels like home. They don't demand transformation; instead, they invite authenticity. Have you ever met someone for the first time and felt as though you'd known them forever? The interaction flows naturally—no rehearsed lines, no awkwardness, just effortless connection. If being with someone requires you to significantly alter who you are, it might be a sign they are not your other half.

The problem is that we often move from one relationship to another carrying our unresolved issues and shortcomings, hoping that these connections will somehow fix us. Instead of working on ourselves, we try to reshape our partners to compensate for our own inner chaos. If you notice yourself repeating the same patterns across different relationships, it's a strong indication that the issue lies within you.

Your past partners would not have treated you in a certain way unless, on some level, you allowed it. For someone to belittle you, there must be something in your demeanor that signals, "I'm a doormat—walk on me." Don't be naïve. In relationships, people treat you according to the standard you set for yourself. You teach others how to treat you by what you tolerate and expect.

The person who truly complements you will have a personality that resonates with yours. To break free from a cycle of unfulfilling relationships, you must begin with honest introspection. This inner exploration leads to a clearer understanding of your deepest thoughts and emotions, shedding light on the truth of your dating patterns through thoughtful reflection on your past experiences.

We choose romantic partners in line with our dating attitude—a mindset shaped by our thoughts and emotions about what it feels like to be in a relationship with a certain kind of person. This attitude influences who we're drawn to and why. When you meet someone who truly fits you, the connection feels natural because your emotional and mental makeup aligns with theirs in a meaningful way.

The Anaclitic Object Choice

In addition to the contributions of ancient Greek philosophers, Sigmund Freud stands out as a major figure in the discussion of romantic choice. His work on human sexuality remains one of the most influential references in the field, making it difficult to approach the subject without acknowledging his theories.

In his 1914 essay *On Narcissism: An Introduction*, Freud introduced the term *anaclitic object choice*, distinguishing it from *narcissistic object choice*. In anaclitic object choice, an individual selects a love object that resembles either the nurturing figure who provided care (such as the mother) or the protective figure who offered safety (such as the father). These choices are modeled on early relationships with parents or parental substitutes.

Freud's idea centers on the notion that romantic or emotional attachments in adulthood are shaped by early dependency needs. People tend to gravitate toward partners who fulfill roles similar to those once occupied by key caregivers. A man who experienced strong emotional bonds with his mother may be drawn to nurturing, maternal partners. Similarly, a woman who relied on her father for emotional security may seek protective and authoritative partners.

Those with insecure or unstable early attachments may face challenges in adult relationships, swinging between intense dependency and fear of abandonment. Freud's theory of anaclitic object choice continues to influence psychoanalytic thinking and has helped lay the foundation for modern attachment theory and the study of romantic relationship dynamics.

Moreover, the concept of anaclitic object choice offers insight into why a nineteen-year-old college student might develop a crush on her math professor who is twenty years older than she is. She's one of the most attractive young women on campus, admired by many of her peers, yet the only person who truly captivates her is the professor. Importantly, her interest isn't driven by financial need—she comes from a well-off, middle-class family that supports her comfortably. So, one might wonder: what could she possibly see in a forty-year-old divorced academic?

What's often overlooked is that the roots of desire and attachment run deeper than what appears on the surface. While most people focus on her feelings for the professor, those who know her family background might better understand where those feelings originate. The concept of anaclitic object choice helps explain this dynamic. Her father and her professor share notable similarities—they are both highly educated, disciplined, and, crucially, her father is also twenty years older than her mother.

Such parallels are not coincidental. We often unconsciously model our romantic preferences on the relationships we observed growing up. The dynamic between her parents has likely influenced her internal blueprint for intimacy. In many ways, her attraction to the professor is not surprising; it reflects a deeply ingrained emotional pattern rooted in her earliest attachments.

The Narcissistic Object Choice

Ten years after introducing the concept of anaclitic object choice, Freud proposed a second form of romantic selection known as narcissistic object choice. In his work *On Narcissism: An Introduction*, he describes this type of sexual choice as one rooted in the individual's relationship with themselves. Rather than seeking partners who meet caregiving or dependency needs, as in anaclitic choice, individuals exhibiting narcissistic object choice are drawn to partners who reflect or enhance their own self-image. They may pursue those who embody an idealized version of themselves or who reinforce their personal aspirations and identity.

This type of object choice also involves certain disruptions in sexual development. Freud believed that disturbances in early psychosexual development could lead to outcomes such as homosexuality or perversions, positioning these within the framework of narcissistic object choice (Freud, 1914).

Freud's theory offers a compelling lens through which to examine how self-perception influences romantic attraction. In narcissistic object choice, the lover is not so much loved for who they are, but for how well they represent the self—or the self as it wishes to be. The romantic partner becomes a mirror, reflecting back an idealized version of the chooser.

Narcissistic lovers often exhibit a grandiose sense of self-importance. They may believe they are too exceptional to engage in relationships with ordinary people. Instead, they seek out partners of high status or perceived superiority, treating them as extensions of their own self-worth. Beneath this inflated self-image, however, lies a fragile core. The grandeur is often a defense mechanism used to mask deep-seated feelings of inadequacy. For such individuals, romantic relationships are less about genuine connection and more about fulfilling fantasies of perfection and self-completion.

Freud's idea that individuals are drawn to reflections of themselves in others challenges traditional views of love as an entirely selfless act. Instead, he suggests that love is at least partially self-referential—driven by a desire to affirm or elevate one's own self-image through the qualities found in a partner. This view is supported by contemporary psychological research indicating that self-esteem significantly influences romantic partner selection (Murray et al., 1996).

However, Freud's perspective also invites important ethical and emotional questions. If one loves another primarily for their similarity to oneself, does this reduce the partner to a mere projection or extension of the ego? Can authentic intimacy exist in a relationship where love serves more to reinforce self-worth than to appreciate the unique individuality of the other? While Freud's theory offers insight into certain patterns of attraction, it may fail to account for the profound emotional bonds that arise from truly recognizing, respecting, and loving a partner not for their resemblance to oneself, but for their distinct "otherness."

The Construct of Anima and Animus

Another significant perspective on the nature of love can be found in the work of Carl Gustav Jung. As the founder of analytical psychology, Jung introduced the concepts of *anima* and *animus* to represent the unconscious feminine side of men and the unconscious masculine side of women. These archetypes, rooted in his theory of the collective unconscious, play a key role in shaping personality, behavior, and romantic attraction (Jung, 1953/1969).

Jung believed that every man carries within him an unconscious feminine aspect—the anima—while every woman possesses an unconscious masculine aspect—the animus. The integration of these inner opposites is essential for psychological growth and self-realization. However, societal expectations about gender roles often discourage individuals from acknowledging traits associated with the opposite sex. As a result, instead of embracing and integrating these qualities into the conscious personality, people tend to repress them into the unconscious.

Jungian psychology holds that elements of the psyche that are not consciously integrated are often projected onto others. In romantic relationships, this projection can manifest as intense attraction, particularly in what is often described as love at first sight. Jungians interpret such sudden and powerful feelings as the projection of the anima or animus onto another person. These inner archetypes carry emotional energy, and when that energy is projected onto someone, it creates the illusion of a profound connection, stirring deep emotional responses that may not be rooted in the actual traits of the person being idealized.

Jung proposed that romantic attraction often arises from projecting one's anima or animus onto another person. In other words, people don't just fall in love with someone else—they fall in love with their own unconscious ideal of femininity or masculinity (Jung, 1969). For instance, a man might project his anima onto a woman who seems nurturing, mysterious, or inspiring, perceiving her not as she truly is but as the embodiment of his internal feminine ideal. Similarly, a woman might project her animus onto a man she sees as powerful, wise, or protective, often elevating him to the status of a hero or authority figure. These projections, while emotionally intense, can set the stage for disappointment when the actual person fails to live up to the imagined ideal (Jung, 1953).

If you take a moment to reflect on your own personal history, you might recall a time—perhaps even now—when you were drawn to someone largely because of how strongly they embodied traits associated with masculinity or femininity. Consider, for example, why many men are attracted to cheerleaders, models, or beauty queens. It's not merely about appearance or sex appeal; rather, it's the symbolic femininity these figures represent. Men, who are often conditioned to repress feminine qualities within themselves, tend to project those qualities onto women. Cheerleaders with their bright outfits, enthusiastic chants, and youthful energy are often seen as representations of beauty, purity, and innocence—qualities men admire but are socially discouraged from associating with themselves.

In the same way, women may be drawn to clean-cut men in suits or uniforms. Despite increasing professional independence and economic success, many women still find themselves attracted to men who exhibit traits of traditional social dominance. This can be understood as the projection of the animus—a yearning for strength, structure, and authority that may mirror unconscious masculine ideals. Whether or not these men truly possess those qualities is beside the point; the emotional impact comes from the internal projection, not the reality of the individual.

Women have traditionally been discouraged from developing traits symbolically associated with masculinity, such as dominance and leadership. As a result, these qualities are often repressed into the unconscious. It follows that many women may feel a strong attraction to individuals who appear to embody those very traits. A well-tailored suit or a distinctive uniform, for instance, can accentuate both social and physical distinctions between the wearer and other men. Military uniforms, in particular, carry an implicit sense of accomplishment—they must be earned and often signify discipline, strength, and authority. These symbols highlight the wearer's elevated status and physical competence, making them especially compelling targets for unconscious projection.

The Imprinting Phenomenon

In discussing sexual attraction, ethologists often refer to a phenomenon known as imprinting. This concept was first identified by Konrad Lorenz through his studies of greylag geese. Imprinting is a rapid form of learning that occurs during a critical period early in life, when a young animal forms a strong and lasting attachment to the first moving object it encounters—typically its mother. Lorenz famously demonstrated this by becoming the object of imprinting for newly hatched goslings, who proceeded to follow him as if he were their biological parent (Lorenz, 1935). This process represents the newborn's initial recognition and bonding with caregivers.

Lorenz's theory of imprinting marked a major advancement in the field of ethology by showing that such attachments are instinctive and largely irreversible when formed during a specific developmental window. While his work focused on animals, the concept has significant implications for human psychology, particularly in the realm of attachment theory.

One of the most important forms of imprinting is filial imprinting, which serves as the foundation for social bonds in young animals. This sensitive period immediately following birth is when an infant forms a deep connection with the most prominent figure in its environment. The emotional attachment formed during this phase plays a crucial role in shaping future social and relational behavior.

One of the most important insights from filial imprinting is its focus on a critical period—a narrow window in early development during which learning occurs rapidly and leaves a lasting impact (Hess, 1958). This idea has had a significant influence beyond ethology, particularly in human psychology. For instance, John Bowlby (1969) adapted the concept to human attachment theory, proposing that early bonds with caregivers play a vital role in shaping emotional and social development throughout life.

In humans, sexual imprinting is often described as the process through which individuals unconsciously model their romantic preferences on the personality traits of their opposite-sex parent. This means romantic choice can represent an unconscious transaction, either healthy or unhealthy, depending on whether the imprinting was positive or negative. Positive sexual imprinting refers to a developmental process in which a person becomes inclined toward partners who share qualities with their opposite-sex parent. Originally observed by Konrad Lorenz (1935) in his studies on greylag geese, imprinting ensures that young animals form a secure bond with their caregiver during a specific, sensitive period, improving their chances of survival. This bond is both rapid and irreversible. Though human bonding is far more nuanced than the instinctual imprinting seen in birds, the principle still applies: early interactions with caregivers shape adult attachment styles and influence romantic partner selection. Recognizing the role of positive imprinting allows for a deeper understanding of how subconscious patterns from childhood affect emotional expectations in adult relationships. With this awareness, individuals may be better equipped to make conscious, healthier choices in love and intimacy.

Positive imprinting influences mate selection in subtle but significant ways, shaped by both biological instincts and social conditioning. Research suggests that early experiences with caregivers leave a subconscious imprint that informs our preferences in romantic partners, including tendencies toward specific physical traits, personality characteristics, and patterns of emotional attachment (Lorenz, 1935). These early influences often guide us toward individuals who unconsciously resemble those who nurtured us during childhood.

In contrast, negative imprinting refers to the development of sexual aversion toward individuals who resemble one's opposite-sex parent or those closely involved during infancy and early childhood. Within the framework of imprinting, sexual attraction is viewed as an innate tendency to seek partners who echo the emotional dynamics of our earliest relationships. However, in cases of negative imprinting, this tendency may result in the rejection of partners who resemble emotionally harmful or distressing figures from one's past. While positive imprinting revives early pleasurable associations, negative imprinting can reflect an unconscious effort to avoid repeating painful emotional experiences.

Negative imprinting arises when early relationships involve neglect, inconsistency, or abuse. These experiences create harmful internal models of attachment, often leading to difficulties in forming secure and healthy bonds later in life. This notion, rooted in Lorenz's (1935) work and expanded by Bowlby's (1969) attachment theory, helps explain why some individuals develop anxious or avoidant attachment styles. Children exposed to unreliable or harmful caregivers may struggle with intimacy, trust, or emotional regulation as adults, frequently repeating dysfunctional patterns in their romantic lives (Ainsworth, 1978).

Understanding negative imprinting highlights the profound and lasting impact of early relational experiences. Although such early influences can set challenging patterns in motion, change is possible. Through self-awareness, reflection, and therapeutic intervention, individuals can begin to unlearn maladaptive behaviors and foster healthier, more secure emotional connections in their adult relationships.

Bowlby's attachment theory (1969) proposes that early interactions with caregivers form internal "working models" that shape expectations and behaviors in later relationships. Individuals who received consistent, nurturing care tend to develop secure attachments and seek out emotionally responsive and dependable partners. Conversely, those who experienced inconsistent or neglectful caregiving may form insecure attachments and be drawn to emotionally unavailable or unpredictable partners, mirroring unresolved patterns from their early life (Hazan & Shaver, 1987).

The influence of opposite-sex parents on mate selection is a powerful and often unconscious force. Early relational experiences significantly impact the types of romantic attraction we develop during adolescence and adulthood (Bowlby, 1969). The foundational dynamics established in childhood frequently guide future preferences, as individuals are often drawn to partners who resemble their opposite-sex parent. For instance, if a woman shares characteristics with a man's mother, he may feel at ease in her presence due to the familiarity she evokes. People tend to gravitate toward familiar stimuli, and this sense of familiarity can make certain individuals more appealing, as they subconsciously recall the comfort and positive emotions associated with early caregiving experiences.

Physical Attractiveness

Physical attractiveness plays a significant role in mate selection, particularly in the early stages of romantic attraction. Beauty functions as a powerful motivator, often shaping how individuals assess the desirability of potential partners. A study conducted at Villanova University found that men whose photographs were rated as physically attractive were also perceived as having more appealing text profiles by women on a dating platform (Brand et al., 2012). This suggests that physical appearance can influence perceptions beyond surface-level traits.

While personality, values, and compatibility remain important, research consistently confirms that physical appearance is among the first qualities considered when selecting a partner. This tendency is rooted in both evolutionary biology and social conditioning. Evolutionary psychology posits that physical attractiveness signals health, fertility, and genetic fitness—traits that historically enhanced reproductive success (Buss, 1989). Features such as facial symmetry, clear skin, and a well-proportioned body are often perceived as indicators of genetic stability and overall health (Rhodes, 2006; Griffiths & Dutton, 2011). Youthfulness is also associated with fertility, leading many individuals to prefer younger partners (Buss & Schmitt, 1993).

Attractive individuals often receive more favorable social treatment, which can enhance their perceived desirability. People may even abandon their usual selection criteria when unexpectedly presented with a particularly attractive potential partner, highlighting the magnetic pull of physical beauty.

Although it is commonly believed that men are more focused on physical appearance than women, research indicates that both sexes respond to visual cues, albeit in different ways. From an evolutionary standpoint, the "good genes" hypothesis suggests that women are drawn to men who display signs of health, strength, and vitality. These traits are associated with genetic quality and the capacity to protect and provide for offspring (Buss, 1989). Thus, both men and women prioritize physical traits that imply reproductive advantage, though their preferences may be shaped by different reproductive strategies.

Certain physical traits in men are commonly interpreted as markers of good health and are often preferred by women during mate selection. Features such as facial symmetry, muscularity, and other indicators of physical fitness are valued because they are believed to reflect strong immune function, fertility, and genetic resilience. Symmetrical facial features, for example, have been consistently linked to perceptions of attractiveness, as they are thought to signal genetic stability and a lower susceptibility to disease (Rhodes, 2006).

Masculine facial features—like a pronounced jawline, defined cheekbones, and a deeper voice—are also associated with higher levels of testosterone. These traits not only suggest reproductive fitness but also influence female perceptions of health and dominance (Penton-Voak et al., 1999). In addition, physical fitness plays a crucial role. Muscular, athletic male bodies with low body fat are perceived as more attractive, partly because they suggest strength and the potential to protect and provide for offspring. Research by Dixson and Brooks (2013) supports this, showing that women are more attracted to men with well-developed musculature as a sign of overall vitality.

However, while physical appearance may initially spark interest, it alone is insufficient to sustain a meaningful emotional connection. Attraction may begin with what pleases the eye, but lasting love depends on deeper psychological and emotional compatibility. Like a plant that requires a specific mix of nutrients—carbon, hydrogen, oxygen, and water—to thrive, love also depends on essential elements drawn from the personalities of both partners.

The emotional depth and longevity of a relationship are rooted in mutual understanding, trust, communication, and shared values. Just as a plant withers without proper nourishment, a relationship that lacks emotional support and psychological compatibility will eventually falter. Ultimately, the success or failure of romantic love depends not just on initial attraction, but on the unique psychological makeup and interpersonal dynamics between the two individuals involved.

The Pathological Aspect of Love

Contrary to the traditional view of love as a clear, rational, and conscious choice, love often reflects our inner psychological imbalances. In fact, romantic attraction frequently stems from unresolved emotional wounds. Our psychological dysfunctions play a surprisingly significant role in shaping who we are drawn to and who is drawn to us. These inner conflicts often dictate the type of partners we pursue and the patterns we repeat in relationships.

In his book *Le Couple Retrouvé* (*The Found Couple*), the German-born French psychologist Patrick Estrade asserts, "It is our neurosis that drives us to love someone" (Estrade, 1991). One doesn't need to be a Freudian to recognize the truth in this statement—our romantic and sexual experiences often validate it. Why are we consistently drawn to certain types of people? Why do we find ourselves repeating the same relationship mistakes? The answer lies in our unaddressed emotional needs. Since many of us have neglected the deeper needs of the soul, falling in love becomes a way to compensate for our inner voids.

To better grasp Estrade's argument, we must first understand what neurosis is. Neurosis refers to a mental or emotional disturbance that isn't caused by any physical or neurological defect. Unlike psychosis, neurosis doesn't involve a complete break from reality but rather a conflicted relationship with it.

A neurotic person experiences an internal battle between unconscious impulses and conscious restraint—between the primal urges of the id and the repressive voice of the superego. This conflict often finds expression in subtle, socially acceptable behaviors rather than overt dysfunction. What distinguishes neurosis from psychosis is awareness: a psychotic may believe they *are* someone else, while a neurotic *wrestles* with the desire to become someone they're not. Common forms of neurosis include anxiety and depression, with symptoms such as obsessive thinking, irritability, perfectionism, low self-esteem, emotional dependency, and suppressed anger.

In many cases, romantic choices are unconsciously shaped by unresolved emotional conflicts within the self. Why are submissive individuals often drawn to authoritarian partners? Why do sadistic and masochistic personalities frequently gravitate toward one another? Intriguingly, we tend to be attracted to people whose psychological dysfunctions mirror or complement our own.

At first glance, it may seem paradoxical that emotional or psychological difficulties could serve as the foundation for romantic attraction. Yet research suggests that unresolved internal struggles often influence the dynamics of romantic relationships, shaping both whom we choose and how we relate to them. This influence operates through various psychological mechanisms, including attachment styles, emotional vulnerability, and trauma bonding. In many cases, individuals subconsciously seek out partners who seem to meet unmet emotional needs or who resonate with familiar—though often dysfunctional—patterns. While these relationships may not always be healthy, they fulfill deep psychological desires for recognition, security, or validation.

One of the most widely studied frameworks for understanding how psychological issues affect romantic attraction is attachment theory, originally developed by John Bowlby (1969). According to this theory, early experiences with caregivers shape internal working models of love and intimacy, which later influence how individuals form and maintain romantic bonds. Emotional wounds rooted in childhood—such as abandonment fears, anxiety, or avoidance—can significantly guide romantic preferences and behaviors. For instance, individuals with an anxious attachment style often crave closeness, reassurance, and emotional validation. They may find themselves drawn to intense, emotionally charged relationships, even when those relationships cause distress (Hazan & Shaver, 1987). This can lead to a cycle of attraction to emotionally unavailable or inconsistent partners, reinforcing dependency and emotional volatility. Conversely, those with an avoidant attachment style tend to fear intimacy and may withdraw emotionally when relationships become too close. Yet paradoxically, they may be drawn to partners who provoke these fears, perpetuating a push-pull dynamic that keeps true intimacy out of reach (Mikulincer & Shaver, 2007).

Ultimately, romantic attraction is not always as conscious or rational as we might like to believe. It is often the reflection of hidden wounds—echoes of the past seeking resolution in the present. Romantic attraction is not always the result of conscious choice or rational thought. More often than we realize, it reflects hidden emotional wounds—echoes of past experiences seeking resolution in the present.

People struggling with psychological difficulties such as depression, anxiety, or low self-esteem often feel emotionally vulnerable and may turn to romantic relationships in search of validation and support. This vulnerability can draw them toward partners who appear to offer emotional rescue, even when such relationships are marked by dependency or dysfunctional patterns (Mikulincer & Shaver, 2007).

Though discomforting, emotional vulnerability can also open the door to intimacy. Individuals who are psychologically fragile may be more receptive to emotional connection and thus more inclined to form close attachments with those who provide empathy and affirmation. Research suggests that those with low self-esteem are particularly attracted to partners who validate their worth. However, this need for affirmation can sometimes lead to attraction toward narcissistic individuals, whose charm and confidence offer temporary boosts in self-worth but often result in toxic relational dynamics (Jonason et al., 2013).

A particularly damaging form of unhealthy attachment is known as trauma bonding—an intense emotional connection that develops between an individual and a harmful or abusive partner. This bond is often reinforced through intermittent reinforcement, a pattern in which periods of kindness and affection are unpredictably interspersed with emotional neglect or abuse (Dutton & Painter, 1981). Despite the pain such relationships cause, the inconsistency can deepen attachment, making it difficult to leave.

Individuals who have experienced early-life trauma, such as childhood abuse or neglect, are especially vulnerable to forming trauma bonds. These people may unconsciously gravitate toward partners whose behavior mirrors the emotional unpredictability they encountered in childhood—alternating between warmth and rejection. In such cases, romantic relationships become an unconscious attempt to resolve unresolved trauma. This often results in repeating familiar but destructive emotional patterns, as originally theorized by Bowlby (1969).

Ultimately, many individuals with psychological struggles seek not just love but healing through their romantic choices—often chasing emotional resolution in the very places where their wounds were first inflicted. To truly understand a person's romantic or sexual preferences is to gain insight into who they are at a core psychological level. The patterns people follow in love—whether consistent or chaotic—often reflect deep emotional conflicts rooted in past experiences. These choices are not merely about attraction or compatibility; they are frequently shaped by unresolved tensions and unconscious needs.

Take, for example, a well-educated man with low self-esteem. He may consistently be drawn to women who are less educated or from a lower socioeconomic background. Outwardly, this preference might seem arbitrary, but subconsciously, such relationships feel safe to him. These women don't threaten his fragile sense of self; in fact, they often reinforce it. In their admiration, he finds a kind of emotional refuge. With them, he is the authority, the intellectual, the provider—their "god," in a sense. Around such women, he doesn't have to wrestle with feelings of inadequacy or fear of rejection. His internal anxieties are calmed, not provoked.

Now consider a different example: the woman at work who constantly boasts about her boyfriend or husband—his degrees, his prestige, his intelligence. Her identity is tethered to his accomplishments. Why? Because he represents borrowed worth. By attaching herself to a man society sees as valuable, she believes she, too, becomes valuable. For her, love is not just emotional—it's compensatory. Her choice of partner helps mask her deep-seated inferiority complex. She may endure emotional neglect or even humiliation to maintain this illusion of value. She tolerates his arrogance and domineering behavior because being with him validates her in the eyes of others—and perhaps, more importantly, in her own.

The neurotic individual, driven by inner anxiety, is often motivated to reduce discomfort in every domain of life—career, social interactions, and especially romance. Each romantic choice is less about desire and more about self-protection. You might wonder what he sees in the partners he consistently chooses. The answer lies not in what he consciously wants, but in what he unconsciously needs: emotional safety. He chooses people who won't awaken the dormant emotional conflicts buried deep in his psyche. His choices are not random—they are survival strategies crafted by his unconscious mind.

No matter how attractive or intelligent a man may appear, if he believes he is undeserving of a confident, high-value partner, he will gravitate toward those who reflect his inner narrative. He may consistently pursue partners who are insecure or less conventionally attractive—not because of a lack of opportunity, but because of an ingrained belief formed long ago. Somewhere in his past, his self-worth was fractured. Perhaps he was told he would never amount to anything. Maybe he faced rejection from a childhood crush or was humiliated by peers during adolescence. These wounds calcify over time, shaping how he sees himself and, inevitably, who he believes he deserves.

There's a French proverb that says, *"A scalded cat fears cold water."* At its core, this saying reflects a deep truth about human behavior: we instinctively avoid situations that remind us of past pain. Our actions, attitudes, and emotional responses are not formed in a vacuum—they are shaped by a lifetime of experiences. Many of those experiences leave behind unresolved emotions that are quietly buried in the subconscious, influencing our choices without our awareness.

This unconscious avoidance is especially evident in our romantic lives. We are often drawn to partners whose personalities or behaviors *won't* trigger repressed feelings rooted in earlier trauma. Take, for example, Heather—a highly educated woman who insists she dates men of lower social status because "there just aren't better prospects" in her area. She may even believe this explanation herself. But deeper down, her behavior reflects something else: fear. Despite the interest of a well-educated co-worker, she avoids him—not because he isn't good enough, but because she believes she isn't. She's convinced that if she were to date him, she would eventually be rejected.

If we could rewind Heather's life, we might find a history marked by emotional rejection or humiliation. Choosing partners she sees as "safe" is her way of protecting herself from re-experiencing those early wounds. Her comfort lies not in compatibility, but in emotional predictability—relationships that won't disturb the delicate balance she's constructed to keep pain at bay.

In fact, most of our choices in life are shaped by one of two motives: to maintain comfort or to minimize anxiety. Our *comfort zone*—far from being simply a space of convenience—is a psychological defense mechanism. It's a set of behaviors and attitudes developed in response to past distress, designed to shield the self from further emotional harm. It's no surprise, then, that many people avoid romantic partners who threaten this mental safe zone.

Heather, for instance, is unlikely to marry a man she fears she could lose to someone "better." Instead, she seeks a partner who places her on a pedestal—someone who worships her. On the surface, there's nothing wrong with being with someone who values and respects you. In fact, it's essential. But when a man sees a woman as a goddess *only* because of his own low self-esteem, the relationship becomes unbalanced. It no longer rests on mutual appreciation, but on one person's need to feel inferior and the other's need to be idealized. In the end, our romantic choices often reflect not just what we want—but what we're afraid to feel again.

The Cinderello Complex

The term "complex" can have various meanings depending on its context, so it's important to place it within the proper framework before defining it. In psychology, a complex refers to a collection of unconscious memories and emotions that shape how we perceive ourselves and others. There are many different types of complexes, and each one reflects a unique psychological pattern. Some of the most well-known complexes in clinical psychology include the Oedipus complex, Electra complex, ego complex, messianic redeemer complex, Cleopatra complex, and Napoleon complex, among others.

The "Cinderello complex," specifically, is a psychological condition that primarily affects men. A man with this complex is often referred to as a "Cinderello." It has no connection to the 2005 Ron Howard film *Cinderella Man*, about boxer James J. Braddock, whose character is fundamentally different from the one described here. Unlike Braddock, who is a hardworking and self-sacrificing man, a Cinderello is someone who believes he deserves to be cared for by women, rather than being an active participant in his own well-being.

A Cinderello's personality could be likened to that of David Edgar Greenhill (a character played by Don Johnson in *Miami Vice*), though without the character's morally questionable traits. A Cinderello, while not as bold as Greenhill in announcing that women should take care of him, holds a similar belief in his own entitlement to special treatment, particularly from women. The Cinderello complex is driven by deep-seated feelings of insecurity and unresolved emotional wounds from childhood, often linked to feelings of inadequacy in comparison to adults or peers. This sense of inferiority is overcompensated by a constant need to feel validated and superior to others.

This type of individual tends to view anyone more successful than himself as a threat and a rival. He might appear outwardly normal, but if you observe the dynamics of his relationships, you would realize he operates in a state of ongoing competition. His relationships, even romantic ones, are often calculated moves designed to bolster his fragile ego. A Cinderello is skilled at forming connections with influential people in his community, whether it's the mayor, local stars, or other prominent figures. He attends important social events and city meetings, always working to ensure that his status and sense of importance are maintained. His life is a game of "battles," and he's constantly strategizing to secure his place in the world.

In reality, a Cinderello is essentially a gigolo in denial, convinced he has dignity and that he would never use his body for financial gain. Though he isn't the type of gigolo you'd find on an escort service website, he behaves much like the masculine equivalent of a gold digger. His primary goal is to extract everything he can from the women he dates. This behavior gives him a sense of inner peace—he believes that a woman who provides for him is simply acknowledging how wonderful he is. For him, choosing a romantic partner becomes a covert strategy to compensate for past social failures, driven by neurotic tendencies or unconscious motives. Being financially supported by a woman boosts his self-worth, offering a way to make up for the deep-seated feelings of inadequacy and worthlessness he harbors.

There is no particular age group for women likely to get involved with Cinderello; they can range from young to old. I once overheard a sixteen-year-old girl lamenting the loss of a boyfriend she used to financially support. To attract or be attracted to a Cinderello, a woman must either be desperate or have low self-esteem. Cinderellos rarely settle down. Most of them are confirmed bachelors who never seem to be satisfied with any of the women they date, always believing they deserve better. They continuously judge their partners, criticizing them for not living up to some idealized standard.

Why Date a Cinderello?

Some women remain in dysfunctional relationships because those environments, paradoxically, validate their own insecurities. To understand this dynamic, romantic attraction can be compared to the growth of a plant. Just as a seed needs the right conditions—nutritious soil, proper light, and water—to flourish, relationships also require a healthy psychological environment to grow. When placed in poor conditions, a seed may sprout but will ultimately struggle to thrive. Likewise, a relationship built in the wrong emotional or psychological climate can become stagnant, toxic, or destructive.

For romantic attraction to take root and endure, there must be a psychological compatibility between partners—a shared emotional landscape that nurtures mutual desire and attachment. Often, this means that the psychological needs, patterns, and even neuroses of both individuals must complement each other. People are unconsciously drawn to partners whose emotional profiles reflect their own unresolved issues, forming what could be called a "mating index"—a subconscious compatibility rooted in shared psychological tendencies. Love is rarely a product of logic; reasoning might explain a connection after the fact, but it's emotion—especially the unconscious kind—that determines attraction.

A common misconception is that women choose to stay with men who are emotionally or financially dependent on them simply because those men are charming, attractive, or sexually satisfying. These so-called "Cinderellos" often believe they are irresistible lovers, confident in their appearance and boasting about their skills in bed. However, beneath this bravado often lies a deep sense of inadequacy. Their charm masks insecurity, and their appeal to certain women is less about charisma and more about emotional codependency.

Women who feel they must earn love through sacrifice—such as financially supporting a partner—may unknowingly reinforce this dynamic. Their insecurity aligns with the man's need for validation, creating a feedback loop in which each partner enables the other's psychological vulnerabilities. In such cases, the relationship thrives not on mutual growth, but on shared dysfunction—a reality that can be hard to break without introspection and healing on both sides.

The Cinderella Complex

In her book *The Cinderella Complex: Women's Hidden Fear of Independence*, Colette Dowling introduces the concept of the Cinderella Complex, which she defines as a subconscious fear of autonomy that affects many women (Dowling, 1981). According to Dowling, this complex leads women to feel most secure when dependent on a powerful man, echoing the fairytale narrative of being rescued by a prince. Most of us have encountered at least one or two "Cinderellas"—women who believe their best chance at success lies in attaching themselves to influential men. Many seem to dream of the ideal partner as a powerful, heroic figure, and when they marry an average man, some feel they've settled or even done him a favor because they believe they deserve a prince.

This desire to be a princess appears to run deep in many women. It helps explain why women, more than men, often focus intensely on their physical appearance. To become more desirable to men, they treat their bodies in specific ways, working out, dieting, or purchasing beauty products in pursuit of a socially-approved ideal. For those who believe that men prefer thin women, gyms and weight-loss products become tools for self-transformation. Historically, beauty has served as a powerful lever for women, especially when access to conventional social or economic power was limited. In response to these constraints, many women have turned to romantic relationships as a path to upward mobility.

Despite modern messages that promote independence and self-determination, many women still hold on to internalized beliefs that link their value to their attractiveness. For the "Cinderellas" in particular, physical beauty remains their most prized asset—a quality they believe is key to securing the affection of a desirable partner. As a result, self-worth for many women becomes closely tied to their appearance, leading to intense dedication to beauty routines and physical maintenance. These efforts, often exhausting and costly, reflect a belief that appearance is not just important—but essential—to their identity and prospects in love.

Despite the progress women have made in challenging male dominance and gaining greater autonomy, many still approach romantic relationships with an underlying desire for social and financial security. If you closely observe their behavior and conversations, you'll often find a subtle, yet persistent, search for a powerful partner under whose protection they can thrive. This drive stems from a deep-rooted belief that fulfillment and happiness are closely tied to securing a high-status mate.

For the woman with a "Cinderella" mindset, failing to marry her ideal "prince" can be a significant emotional blow. In response, she may publicly idealize her "second choice" partner, exaggerating his virtues to compensate for her unfulfilled aspirations. This overcompensation is less about genuine admiration for the partner and more about preserving her self-image. Ultimately, the pursuit of the charming prince is not just about finding love—it's about validation. The prince's appeal lies in the way he elevates her perception of herself. She desires him not just for who he is, but for how he makes her feel about who she is.

A Quest Toward Complementarity

Contrary to popular belief, similarity isn't always the main driver of romantic attraction. While it's often assumed that people are drawn to those who resemble them in values, interests, or background, real-life experience suggests otherwise—it's frequently the differences between individuals that spark the strongest attraction. Many people enter romantic relationships not because they see a mirror image of themselves, but because they sense something is missing in their own lives and believe another person can help fill that void.

This pursuit of love is, in many ways, a quest for self-completion. People commonly express that they're looking for someone to make them feel whole—someone whose presence offsets their personal limitations. In this light, romantic relationships become a dynamic exchange of strengths and weaknesses, where each partner provides what the other lacks.

The notion that we seek partners who "complete us" is deeply ingrained in cultural narratives—from fairy tales to Hollywood films—and reflects a widespread psychological reality. This drive stems from core human needs: attachment, identity reinforcement, and emotional support. From both a psychological and evolutionary standpoint, the desire for a partner who balances or complements our traits is a natural response to the human yearning for security, growth, and connection. We don't just want a partner who is similar—we want someone who makes us feel more like our best selves.

Psychological and Evolutionary Perspectives

From a psychological standpoint, the notion of seeking a partner who "completes" us aligns with the theory of complementary needs. Individuals are often drawn to partners whose traits balance or counterbalance their own, fulfilling emotional or psychological gaps that they cannot meet alone. This dynamic is closely linked to attachment theory (Bowlby, 1969), which posits that people form relationships in part to satisfy fundamental needs for security, connection, and emotional regulation.

Research by Winch (1958) also supports the idea that people are attracted to complementary traits in others. For example, an anxious individual might be soothed by a calm, grounded partner, or an extroverted person may feel grounded by someone more introverted and reflective. These complementary dynamics can provide a sense of emotional equilibrium, as each partner contributes qualities the other may lack.

This desire for psychological balance also connects with the self-concept and the pursuit of wholeness. According to self-expansion theory (Aron & Aron, 1986), individuals are motivated to enter relationships that help them grow by broadening their experiences, perspectives, and sense of identity. A romantic partner who complements us not only meets emotional needs but also facilitates personal development, helping us become fuller versions of ourselves.

In this view, romantic relationships are not just about emotional fulfillment but also about identity enhancement. The right partner becomes a catalyst for self-discovery and actualization, offering the support and stimulus needed to grow beyond one's current limitations

Carl Jung's concept of *individuation*—the integration of unconscious and conscious aspects of the self—proposes that individuals are often drawn to partners who reflect or embody parts of themselves they have not yet fully acknowledged or accepted. These relationships can serve as a mirror, facilitating personal growth and psychological integration, ultimately fostering a deeper sense of wholeness (Jung, 1953).

For many, the belief that a romantic partner can "complete" them stems from a deep emotional need for fulfillment. This fulfillment includes essential psychological needs such as love, validation, support, and companionship. Often, people seek partners who can help resolve unmet emotional needs rooted in childhood or past relationships. In this way, a partner becomes a symbolic figure—someone who fills internal emotional voids and provides a sense of completeness.

Research supports this idea by highlighting the human need for emotional support and belonging, which significantly influences mate selection. Individuals who struggle with feelings of loneliness, rejection, or low self-worth are more likely to pursue relationships that promise emotional security and connection (Cohen & Wills, 1985). These dynamics contribute to the perception that a romantic partner can "complete" one's emotional life.

Additionally, the cultural narrative of being "completed" by a partner has been heavily shaped by romantic idealism portrayed in media. Films, novels, and television often depict love as a magical solution to personal struggles, reinforcing the belief that the right partner can solve emotional problems or bring lasting happiness. While compelling, these ideals may foster unrealistic expectations about relationships and the extent to which they can truly fulfill us.

Kelley and Thibaut (1978) suggest that people often idealize romantic relationships, viewing them as the key to happiness and personal fulfillment. This romanticized belief leads many to expect that a partner will provide a sense of completeness, a notion that is continually reinforced by cultural messages portraying love as life's ultimate achievement.

From the perspective of evolutionary psychology, the desire for a partner who "completes" us can be interpreted as a strategic response to biological and reproductive needs. In this framework, individuals are drawn to mates whose traits and resources complement their own, thereby enhancing the chances of reproductive success and offspring survival. These complementary resources may include emotional stability, parental investment, physical health, or genetic compatibility.

Trivers' (1972) theory of parental investment underscores this dynamic by explaining that men and women have evolved different mating strategies based on their reproductive roles. Women, who bear the greater biological cost of childbearing and nurturing, are evolutionarily inclined to seek partners who can provide long-term support, protection, and stability. Men, on the other hand, may prioritize indicators of fertility and reproductive health, such as youth and physical attractiveness. In both cases, mate selection is driven by the pursuit of traits that complement one's own, optimizing reproductive and relational outcomes.

Moreover, the idea of being "completed" by a partner can be linked to genetic complementarity. Studies have shown that people are often subconsciously attracted to those with differing immune system genes, such as variations in the major histocompatibility complex (MHC), which can result in healthier, more resilient offspring (Schaal et al., 1997). This unconscious biological drive contributes to the sense that an ideal partner offers something we inherently lack—whether emotionally, psychologically, or genetically—thereby "completing" us.

Interpersonal Theory of Personality

A compelling perspective on complementary romantic relationships is the idea that an individual's personality can predict the personality type of their ideal partner. This concept aligns with Robert Carson's "interpersonal theory of personality," specifically the principle of complementarity. According to this principle, a person's behavior naturally elicits certain responses from others, creating self-reinforcing interpersonal dynamics. In romantic relationships, this often means that dominant personalities are drawn to submissive partners and vice versa.

Dominant or controlling individuals tend to gravitate toward partners who are more passive or dependent. This dynamic allows the dominant partner to maintain control and assume a position of authority, often under the guise of protection or guidance. Their psychological comfort stems from being needed, from making decisions, and from holding power in the relationship.

However, beneath the surface of dominance lies deep insecurity. For many controlling individuals, dominating others serves as a defense mechanism to mask feelings of inferiority or low self-worth. Their need to control is less about confidence and more about managing the anxiety that comes from internal instability. In this sense, controlling behavior becomes a coping strategy—a way to avoid confronting their own vulnerabilities.

In relationships, these individuals may choose partners who are emotionally or psychologically dependent in order to feel a sense of superiority. This dynamic feeds their neurotic needs, allowing them to feel powerful and significant. Unfortunately, such individuals may also resort to belittling their partners through dismissive or degrading comments, falsely believing that diminishing others enhances their own value.

At its core, choosing a partner becomes a compensatory act—a subconscious strategy to soothe unresolved inner tensions. When driven by neurosis rather than genuine emotional connection, such relationships often create cycles of dysfunction, where power imbalances replace mutual respect and affection.

Maintaining a healthy relationship requires both partners to willingly engage in rational and conscious compromises—each giving up something to gain something more valuable in return. However, individuals with controlling tendencies often approach relationships not through thoughtful negotiation, but through the lens of unresolved unconscious conflicts. Their decisions are typically not guided by reason or emotional intelligence, but by impulsive inner drives. These individuals tend to be drawn to partners they perceive as inferior, choosing relationships where they can feel superior or indispensable. They want to be seen as saviors—rescuers of someone else's brokenness—which serves to elevate their own fragile self-image.

A hallmark of such relationships is the belief that, when looking at their partner, they should be able to say, "I can do better." Their ideal partner is someone who boosts their sense of superiority while tolerating their ego-driven need to dominate. For the relationship to "work," the partner must not only accept being emotionally uplifted by the controlling individual but also endure the egotism and control tactics that come with it.

There's a common assumption that heterosexual relationships typically operate under a male-dominant/female-submissive structure. While this may be historically or culturally prevalent, the dynamics of dominance and submission in relationships are far more nuanced. Being in charge does not necessarily mean being domineering. Control within a relationship can be mutual, practical, and even necessary—distinct from oppressive behavior.

In fact, in many romantic partnerships, women often take charge of the day-to-day management of the relationship or household. Society frequently delegates the administrative and emotional labor of family life to women, giving them a form of authority that's often overlooked. This dynamic reflects competence rather than control, and organization rather than domination.

Moreover, individuals with strong administrative or leadership skills may naturally assume roles that require directing others. Conversely, people who are more comfortable in supportive roles tend to exhibit submissive behaviors across different types of relationships—not just romantic ones. At some level, all intimate partnerships involve elements of leadership and support, direction and cooperation. This interplay of dominance and submission is less about power and more about compatibility and roles negotiated over time.

Masculinity and femininity, as culturally defined, have long been seen as opposing forces, but healthy relationships thrive when partners recognize and balance their differences, rather than using them to assert control or superiority.

The Rediscovery of Self

"Who am I then? Tell me that first, and then, if I like being that person, I'll come up: if not, I'll stay down here till I'm somebody else." Lewis Carroll, Alice's Adventures in Wonderland (Carroll, 1865).

When searching for love, people often dream of finding the "complete package"—someone who fulfills all their expectations. Before we even begin the search, we usually have a mental image of our ideal partner, including their appearance, intellect, and social status. In essence, we believe we know exactly what we're looking for. This idea closely mirrors the myth told by Aristophanes in Plato's *Symposium*.

If you recall, Aristophanes describes an ancient time when humans were androgynous beings—creatures with one body, two faces, four arms, and four legs. These powerful beings dared to challenge the gods, and as punishment, Zeus split them in half, creating the separate sexes. Since that division, humans have been driven by a deep yearning to find their missing half—a longing that Aristophanes identifies as Eros, the force of love. Love, then, is not just about desire; it is a quest for wholeness.

Finding that special person—the one who sets your heart on fire and makes you feel complete—often feels like rediscovering a lost part of yourself. Have you ever met someone for the first time, yet felt as though you've known them forever? Have you experienced love at first sight? People often enjoy sharing how they met their partner. Maybe it was in a park, at a bustling airport, in a church, or during a random meeting where, suddenly, your eyes met and something just clicked. You felt drawn to that stranger, as if led by some invisible thread. Conversation flowed easily, laughter came naturally, and even the smallest gestures felt magical. Others might call it odd, but to you, it simply felt like compatibility—like coming home.

At the core of every human being is a deep desire for wholeness. This drive shapes our romantic pursuits, compelling us to confront our inner needs and yearnings. Often, we are attracted to people who embody traits we lack—qualities that fill our emotional or psychological gaps. According to Aron and Aron's (1986) *self-expansion model*, we grow and enrich our sense of self through close relationships, especially with partners who bring complementary qualities into our lives. By including such individuals in our sense of self, we expand our identity and move closer to becoming whole.

Relationships are not solely about emotional connection—they are also powerful vehicles for personal growth. When we fall in love or form deep bonds with another person, we begin to integrate aspects of them into our own identity. Their traits, perspectives, and experiences can become part of our evolving self, expanding our self-concept and allowing us to grow in ways we may never have achieved alone.

When two people bring different yet complementary strengths to a relationship, each partner has the opportunity to develop through the influence of the other. Rather than seeking someone to "complete" us in a dependent or compensatory way, we naturally evolve by incorporating the best parts of our partner into our sense of self. This is why falling in love often feels transformative—not merely because of emotional intensity, but because love expands who we are at our core.

In its highest form, love serves as a catalyst for self-discovery. It becomes a pathway through which we can rediscover our "whole self." A romantic relationship, especially with someone who differs from us in meaningful ways, becomes a powerful means of achieving self-enhancement and personal integration. Without authentic love, it can be difficult to transcend the limitations imposed by our cultural background or early conditioning. True intimacy fosters a spiritual and emotional exchange in which each partner's inner world becomes embedded in the other's. Over time, this shared connection can reshape how individuals see themselves, helping them develop deeper self-awareness and emotional resilience.

Romantic attraction, then, is not merely a matter of "opposites attract"—it is about the deeper need for self-fulfillment. Often, we are drawn to those who can help us reconcile with unresolved inner conflicts or unmet needs from the past. Each person carries a unique psychological makeup, a composite of past experiences, beliefs, and desires. These elements radiate outward in the form of subtle signals—signals that resonate with others whose psychological profiles are compatible. In this way, love becomes a mutual recognition of kindred souls seeking growth, wholeness, and healing.

Falling in love involves a certain kind of compatibility—but not necessarily the surface-level compatibility of personality traits. Rather than simply a match in character, it may be more accurate to speak of a *compatibility of life experience.* Being an introvert doesn't inherently attract an extrovert. In fact, your need for solitude might frustrate someone who thrives on social interaction and constant engagement. What truly shapes romantic compatibility is not personality alone, but the environment in which each person was shaped—the life experiences, struggles, and emotional landscapes they carry with them.

For example, someone who tolerates repeated emotional abuse in a relationship may not do so out of weakness, but because they have been conditioned—often unconsciously—by past experiences to equate love with pain. A person cannot become a masochist without specific formative events influencing their perception of intimacy and self-worth. Similarly, an abuser's behavior may stem from having been abused themselves, continuing the cycle of trauma. As the saying goes, "Man is a product of his past." To truly understand why two people remain in a painful, destructive relationship, one must explore the psychological and emotional roots that shaped them long before they met.

To some extent, love has the unique capacity to draw out the *authentic self*—the unfiltered, often hidden core of who we are. In romantic relationships, we are exposed emotionally in ways we often are not in other areas of life. The authentic self includes both the conscious and subconscious parts of our being. Some people never realize they have a temper until a relationship provokes it. All it takes is a partner with a neurotic or dysfunctional trait that resonates with your own repressed tendencies. You may not even be aware of these latent parts of yourself until your so-called "soulmate"—the one whose inner dysfunction mirrors your own—enters your life.

The presence of a psychologically "compatible" partner can bring what is hidden into the light. Latent traits—both positive and negative—rise to the surface. What was once buried in the unconscious begins to influence behavior and self-perception. In this way, relationships can be mirrors that reflect not just who we are, but who we have the potential to become—for better or worse.

If you find yourself repeatedly drawn into unhealthy or unfulfilling relationships, it may be a sign that something unresolved within you is seeking expression or resolution. When we enter into romantic relationships, we don't come in as blank slates. We bring our fears, insecurities, past wounds, and longings with us. Until these are acknowledged and addressed, they will continue to shape the choices we make—and the people we choose.

Falling in love is often an unconscious attempt to heal old emotional wounds. However, instead of seeking partners who offer genuine emotional growth and healing, we frequently fall into destructive cycles—leaving one toxic relationship only to find ourselves in another that feels painfully familiar. These repetitive patterns stem from unresolved inner conflicts, and until we become aware of the unconscious motives driving our choices, we remain trapped in the same emotional loops.

Self-awareness is the key to breaking free from these cycles. When you begin to understand the hidden forces that shape your behavior and attractions, you gain the power to make more conscious and healthier relationship choices. Without this inner clarity, any change can feel hollow and uncertain, leaving you questioning your decisions. But as your self-understanding deepens, so does your ability to recognize the kinds of relationships that genuinely serve your growth and emotional well-being. This awareness fosters emotional freedom—liberating you from patterns that no longer serve you and empowering you to seek fulfilling connections.

Many of us are so eager to make a good impression on potential partners that we lose ourselves in the process. Despite the common advice to "just be yourself," we often feel internal pressure to perform—to act like someone we believe the other person will find more appealing. In doing so, we may end up in relationships with people who never truly knew us to begin with. Over time, this disconnect creates emotional distance and disillusionment.

In countless divorce proceedings today, the most common reasons cited are "irreconcilable differences" or "incompatibility." It often raises the question: what drew these individuals together in the first place? Weren't those very differences once part of the attraction? If so, why do they later become sources of conflict? The truth is, it's not our *differences* that lead to disillusionment—it's our *hidden compatibilities*. The unconscious traits we share with our partner—especially the unresolved, dysfunctional ones—can eventually mirror back to us what we haven't yet resolved in ourselves, turning attraction into aversion.

In our rush to find someone who "completes" us, we often mistake illusion for reality. Many fall for someone's projection of who they *want* to be, rather than who they truly are. And while the truth inevitably reveals itself over time, by then, the emotional investment may be too deep to escape without pain. Recognizing this tendency is the first step toward building authentic, emotionally honest relationships—ones in which you are not only seen, but truly known.

The Narcissistic Love Object Choice

Many of us are familiar with the myth of Narcissus—a young man so captivated by his own beauty that he refused to accept any lover unless they matched his perceived perfection. To prompt self-reflection, the gods sent him to Mount Helicon. There, a nymph named Echo fell deeply in love with him, but he rejected her, leaving her to suffer in isolation. Meanwhile, Narcissus became obsessed with his own reflection in a pool of water, so much so that he eventually withered away and died, unable to look away from himself.

This tale stands in stark contrast to the *self-expansion model* of love, which views relationships as a path to personal growth and integration of the other into the self. Narcissus, however, remains locked within the confines of his own ego—his love is not a bridge to another, but a closed loop of self-adoration. True love, by contrast, involves seeing and valuing another person as distinct and meaningful, not simply as a reflection of one's own desires or insecurities. In this light, we might ask: is love a mirror that reflects us, a window that opens us to someone else, or a prison that traps us within ourselves? The answer lies in whether love leads to expansion or entrapment.

In modern relationships, we often see echoes of Narcissus's dilemma—a kind of "Narcissus effect" where love becomes entangled with self-image, validation, and performance rather than genuine emotional connection. Social media, dating culture, and societal pressures have fueled this tendency, turning romantic interactions into curated displays and ego-driven exchanges. Love, for many, has become a way to affirm identity rather than to foster mutual growth.

If all narcissists were as self-contained as the mythical Narcissus—consumed by themselves to the point of collapse—the damage would be self-inflicted. But real-life narcissism is far more insidious. Narcissistic individuals often channel their emotional energy into relationships, not for love's sake, but for unconscious, self-serving reasons. Some narcissistic men, plagued by low self-worth, seek out vulnerable women as a means of boosting their own ego. Similarly, some women lacking self-confidence may seek validation not through personal achievements, but by attaching themselves to high-status or admired partners.

In both cases, love becomes a tool for self-repair, rather than a space for mutual discovery and emotional truth. Recognizing these patterns can help us move away from performative love and toward connections grounded in authenticity, empathy, and shared growth.

A narcissistic lover is often defined by self-centeredness, a heightened sense of superiority, and a striking lack of empathy. While they may initially appear charming, charismatic, and attentive, the relationship often deteriorates as manipulative and emotionally exploitative behaviors emerge. To fully grasp the nature of a narcissistic romantic partner, it's essential to explore not only the traits of narcissism but also the underlying attachment styles and their overall impact on relationship dynamics.

Narcissism exists on a spectrum—from common self-involved tendencies to the more severe and diagnosable Narcissistic Personality Disorder (NPD), as outlined in the *Diagnostic and Statistical Manual of Mental Disorders* (American Psychiatric Association, 2013). Individuals high in narcissistic traits tend to prioritize their image and needs above those of their partner, struggle with genuine emotional intimacy, and frequently engage in controlling or manipulative behaviors to maintain a sense of dominance and admiration.

One of the hallmark traits of narcissistic individuals is grandiosity—the belief in their own superiority and the expectation of special treatment (Miller et al., 2017). In relationships, this often translates into a strong sense of entitlement: their opinions must prevail, their needs come first, and their desires are to be met without question. This mindset creates an imbalance, in which the non-narcissistic partner is constantly expected to provide affirmation, support, and emotional caretaking without reciprocity.

The narcissist's relentless need for admiration can create a dynamic that is emotionally exhausting for their partner. This validation-seeking behavior is not simply about attention—it serves to uphold their fragile self-image (Campbell & Foster, 2007). As a result, the relationship may feel increasingly one-sided, with the partner cast in the role of a cheerleader or caretaker rather than an equal.

Perhaps most damaging is the narcissist's profound lack of empathy. They often fail to connect with or acknowledge their partner's emotions, leading to behaviors that are emotionally dismissive, invalidating, or outright exploitative (Watson et al., 1984). This emotional disconnect paves the way for manipulative tactics, such as:

Gaslighting: Undermining the partner's perception of reality.

Love-bombing: Showering the partner with affection early on, only to withdraw or devalue them later.

Silent treatment: Withdrawing communication as a form of punishment or control.

These patterns foster instability and confusion in the relationship, keeping the partner emotionally off-balance and often dependent on the narcissist's approval.

In essence, relationships with narcissistic individuals are marked by emotional volatility, inequality, and a persistent erosion of the partner's sense of self. Recognizing these patterns is the first step toward setting healthy boundaries or breaking free from harmful dynamics.

Attachment theory offers a powerful lens through which to understand why narcissistic individuals often struggle to maintain healthy romantic relationships. Many narcissists display an avoidant attachment style, characterized by a fear of emotional closeness and a tendency to withdraw when intimacy deepens (Brunell & Campbell, 2011). While they may appear warm, attentive, and charming early in a relationship, this persona often fades as their partner's emotional needs increase. At that point, they may become distant, critical, or emotionally unavailable. This pattern can often be traced back to early childhood experiences where their emotional needs were ignored, dismissed, or inconsistently met, leading them to adopt a defensive stance of emotional self-reliance (Bartholomew & Horowitz, 1991).

Some narcissists—particularly those with vulnerable narcissism—exhibit a disorganized attachment style, which involves a conflicted mix of craving intimacy while simultaneously fearing it (Dickinson & Pincus, 2003). This creates an unstable "push-and-pull" dynamic in their relationships, where they may idealize their partner one moment and devalue them the next. The unpredictable shifts in attention and affection can leave their partner confused, anxious, and constantly trying to win back the narcissist's approval. Narcissists are often drawn to partners who boost their ego, validate their self-worth, and do not challenge their authority or independence (Foster et al., 2003).

Being in a relationship with a narcissist can be emotionally draining and psychologically damaging. One of the most insidious dynamics is intermittent reinforcement—the repeated cycle of affection followed by emotional withdrawal (Tennov, 1979). This cycle keeps the non-narcissistic partner emotionally hooked, hoping for the return of the idealized love that was initially shown. Over time, this leads to emotional dependency, diminished self-esteem, and deep self-doubt. The partner is left constantly striving to meet the narcissist's ever-shifting expectations, usually without receiving adequate emotional support or validation in return (Kohut, 1971).

Narcissistic individuals tend to pursue relationships primarily to maintain and enhance their self-image. They are attracted to partners who they perceive as status-enhancing—people who can reflect well on them or feed their need for admiration. Love, for them, is transactional. As long as the partner serves as a source of validation or resources—emotional, social, or material—the narcissist may appear engaged. But once that utility fades, so does their affection. Their entire social world is built around sustaining their inflated self-image. Consequently, they often show little awareness of, or concern for, their partner's emotional needs or desires.

Initially, narcissists may seem magnetic—exuding confidence, charm, and ambition. These traits are highly attractive and can make people fall for them quickly.

However, with time, the darker aspects of their personality emerge: emotional coldness, manipulation, and a lack of genuine empathy. Once exposed, the very traits that once captivated others can become deeply off-putting, even repulsive.

Freud proposed that every individual's earliest love objects are twofold: the self and the maternal figure, typically the one who provides care and nurturance. From this foundation, he theorized that narcissists select love objects based on self-reference—they are drawn to individuals who mirror aspects of themselves. This may include who they are, who they once were, or who they aspire to become. In narcissistic relationships, the dynamic often involves one partner functioning as an extension of the other's identity. What attracts a narcissist is not necessarily the uniqueness of the other, but the way that person represents the narcissist's idealized self.

Everyone, regardless of their mental health, possesses an internal vision of their ideal self—a version of themselves they are striving to become. However, when someone chooses a romantic partner primarily because that person embodies traits or ideals they lack—and instead of working toward those traits independently— they are engaging in a form of pathological projection. The more unconscious a person is of their psychological deficits, the more likely they are to externalize those deficits, seeking them out in others rather than confronting them within.

Ideally, individuals should have a solid understanding of their own identity before entering into a romantic relationship. Yet many people lack self-awareness, and this ignorance can be a major source of relational dysfunction. Narcissists, like everyone else, seek growth through romantic relationships—but for them, "growth" takes on a distorted meaning. Rather than cultivating self-development, narcissistic individuals pursue relationships as a means of fulfilling grandiose self-images. By partnering with someone who possesses traits they covet, narcissists vicariously claim those traits as their own.

In contrast, emotionally grounded individuals may also be drawn to partners who balance their weaknesses, but they maintain a clear sense of self and respect the other person's individuality. Narcissists do not. Driven by fragile egos, they crave emotional balance and stability—but they try to achieve it through manipulation. Their strategy involves selecting partners who can serve as "narcissistic supplies"—sources of validation, admiration, and reinforcement of their inflated self-concept.

To become attractive to a narcissistic lover, a person must play a specific role: they must act as an accessory to the narcissist's self-image. That means reinforcing the narcissist's belief in their specialness, importance, or superiority. Narcissistic lovers in romantic relationships typically fall into two categories: "self-erasing" and "entitled."

Self-Erasing Strategies

Many of us have encountered—or at least heard of—the story of a highly educated, ambitious woman who repeatedly finds herself in relationships with men who lack direction, motivation, or a clear vision for their future. Despite holding a college degree and envisioning a life with a professional partner who shares her intellectual and career goals, she continually dates men who are aimless, underachieving, and emotionally dependent. Time and again, she becomes involved with men who have little education or ambition, often those who never completed a degree or even dropped out of high school.

Her relationships follow a familiar pattern. She immerses herself in her partner's life, attempting to mold him into her ideal vision of success. Reflecting on her most recent breakup, she might say, *"Being with him was like going back to college. I took him to the library, did the research, and even wrote his papers—just so he could get his life together. I gave everything of myself for him."* On the surface, her efforts appear selfless, even noble. But beneath this self-sacrificing façade lies a deeper, unconscious motive: she isn't helping him as much as she is trying to fulfill her own narcissistic needs.

This self-erasing behavior serves two primary narcissistic purposes. First, by "saving" someone, she boosts her own self-esteem—proving her value through someone else's transformation. Second, by attempting to turn these men into the successful, professional partners she dreams of, she seeks to validate her self-worth and soothe her deep-seated insecurities. If she can shape a man into someone society respects, it reflects positively on her.

To the untrained eye, her pattern of self-denial may seem altruistic, even romantic. But in truth, it's a calculated strategy designed to extract admiration, loyalty, and dependence. Narcissistic individuals who use self-erasing strategies aim to be adored—if not idolized—by their partners. The praise and gratitude they anticipate receiving reinforce their inflated self-image and sense of control.

Furthermore, narcissists who adopt the self-erasing persona often disguise their need for dominance behind gestures of caretaking. They don't accept others as they are; instead, they attempt to reshape them to serve their emotional needs. In her case, the men she chooses are not allowed to simply be themselves—they are expected to fulfill a role in her personal narrative. Their success is engineered not for their benefit, but to enhance her identity and elevate her social standing.

Ultimately, her relationships are not partnerships—they are projects. And the people she dates are not partners—they are mirrors meant to reflect back her ideal self. Her feeling of worth depends on maintaining relationships with those she perceives as beneath her, so she can continue to position herself as superior and indispensable. What appears to be compassion is, in reality, a strategy for drawing attention, admiration, and a sense of control.

The Entitled Lover

Entitled lovers are exploitative individuals who enter romantic relationships primarily for personal gain. Rather than seeking connection, intimacy, or mutual growth, they are driven by the desire to enhance their self-image through association with socially elevated or powerful partners. Their sense of entitlement compels them to choose love interests based on status, wealth, influence, or public recognition—not emotional compatibility.

What sets entitled lovers apart from self-erasing narcissists is the transparency of their motives. While self-erasing individuals mask their self-centeredness behind a façade of self-sacrifice and helpfulness, entitled lovers are far more overt in their pursuit of admiration and validation. Their egocentric tendencies are often unmistakable. For them, a romantic relationship serves as confirmation of their fantasies of superiority and uniqueness—a way to camouflage deep-rooted feelings of inadequacy.

Consider the story of a woman now in her second marriage. She has two children—one from each union—and has consistently pursued high-status men. Her first husband was a politician; her second, a well-known athlete. Even in high school, she exclusively dated the most socially prominent boys—the lead singer of the school band, the quarterback, and the editor of the school newspaper. To the outside world, she seems to be living a dream: married to a wealthy, attractive man, residing in an affluent neighborhood, supported by household staff, and sending her children to elite private schools.

Yet beneath the surface, she remains unfulfilled. Her narcissistic fantasies prevent her from experiencing the deeper happiness that comes with mutual love and emotional commitment. Despite the image of perfection, her marriage is unraveling. She and her husband have begun therapy to assess whether the relationship can be salvaged. In their first session, the husband confesses, "I don't recognize her anymore. She's not the woman I married two years ago. Back then, she was everything I dreamed of—understanding, affectionate, patient, even forgiving when I missed a date. She was stunning and compassionate, like Angelina Jolie with the heart of Mother Teresa."

But what her husband didn't realize is that this idealized version of her was a carefully constructed persona, crafted to lure him in. Like many entitled lovers, she knew exactly how to present herself to secure a partner who could reinforce her self-worth. Once the relationship was established, and her need for status and validation was temporarily fulfilled, her emotional investment waned. The romantic gestures weren't acts of love but tactics of manipulation. She wasn't connecting with him—she was performing for him.

Entitled narcissists do not truly love, nor do they expect genuine love in return. Their partners serve a function: to feed their fragile egos and affirm their inflated self-concept. When a partner begins to voice dissatisfaction or pull away, narcissists often react not with introspection, but with confusion or blame. The idea that love might require mutual care and vulnerability is foreign to them. For entitled lovers, the relationship is a transaction—if it no longer provides narcissistic "supplies," then it's deemed defective.

To maintain control, entitled narcissists routinely engage in manipulative behaviors. When their attempts to influence or dominate a partner fail, they perceive it not as a cue to change but as a flaw in the other person or the relationship itself. Their emotional immaturity and rigid entitlement make authentic connection nearly impossible. What appears to be love is often just a mirror reflecting their own unfulfilled ambitions and insecurities.

Parental Image and Romantic Choice

The idea that we choose romantic partners based on parental images is a well-established concept in psychology and evolutionary theory. This phenomenon suggests that our early experiences with caregivers, particularly our parents, shape our perceptions of love, attraction, and compatibility later in life. Theories such as Freudian psychoanalysis, attachment theory, and imprinting theory provide valuable insights into how parental relationships influence our mate selection.

From a psychological perspective, we often use our parental image as a template when choosing love interests. The foundation of romantic love begins not at the first infatuation but during infancy. The mother, as the primary caregiver, represents the first love object in a child's life. In most cases, she is the one who nurtures, feeds, and protects, making her the first person from whom the infant receives comfort and affection. Therefore, the infant naturally forms an attachment to the person who fulfills these early emotional needs.

Sigmund Freud (1927) proposed that individuals unconsciously seek partners who resemble their opposite-sex parent. His theories on the Oedipus complex in boys and the Electra complex in girls suggest that children experience unconscious desires for their opposite-sex parent while competing for the affection of their same-sex parent. Freud (1920) argued that people subconsciously seek relationships that mirror their early parental dynamics, even if those relationships were problematic. This theory posits that the bonds formed with parents significantly influence who we are drawn to in adulthood—physically and emotionally—often replicating the early attachment patterns, whether healthy or not.

As children grow, they begin to identify with their same-sex parent. Girls, for example, start to model themselves after their mothers and become more interested in potential male partners. Boys, on the other hand, identify with their fathers and start to seek relationships with girls their own age. The love we feel in romantic relationships can be seen as a rekindling of the comfort we first experienced with our mothers. Doesn't the presence of the person we love bring us a sense of security? Just as the mother alleviates biological tensions like hunger and thirst, a lover provides emotional and sexual comfort.

Love, in its essence, is an investment in which we seek excitement, pleasure, and fulfillment. While we may not always admit it, what we often seek in love is the kind of nurturing, motherly comfort we once received as children. Just as a mother alleviates physical discomfort, a romantic partner helps us cope with emotional and sexual tensions, offering relief from the loneliness and uncertainty we sometimes face.

The attachment we form with our mothers or primary caregivers serves as a blueprint for future relationships. The emotional bonds established in infancy create "internal working models" of self and others, which shape how we engage in adult relationships. These early experiences influence our emotional responses and perceptions in later romantic connections. Therefore, the dynamics established in childhood form the basis for the types of relationships we develop as adults.

The connection between parental images and romantic attraction has been supported by various scholars and researchers. Freud's theory of anaclitic object choice (1914) suggests that individuals choose partners who resemble their opposite-sex parents. Modern scientific studies support this idea. For instance, a study conducted by Bereczkei (2009) at the University of Pécs in Hungary found that people are likely to choose romantic partners who bear a striking resemblance to their opposite-sex parent. The study measured the facial proportions of 312 adults from 52 families and found a significant correlation between the facial features of male participants and the fathers of their romantic partners, as well as similar correlations for female participants and their mothers.

Another significant study, titled *Perceived and Actual Characteristics of Parents and Partners: A Test of a Freudian Model of Mate Selection* (Little et al., 2004), examined whether parental image truly influences mate selection. Participants were asked to describe the personalities of their parents and romantic partners, and their parents and partners also described themselves. The results revealed that participants' romantic partners often shared similar personality traits with their opposite-sex parent, and that relationship satisfaction was significantly linked to the degree of perceived similarity between parents and partners.

The environment in which we grow up plays a crucial role in shaping our preferences in partners. As previously mentioned, the relationship dynamics between parents and children influence the romantic patterns we develop as adults. Our first experiences with love—whether positive or negative—become models for how we relate to others. The way our parents love and care for us sets the benchmarks for how we engage in romantic relationships. A healthy relationship with a parent of the opposite sex is crucial for the success of our adult love lives.

When we reflect on our own romantic histories, we may realize that many of the people we have dated or loved share characteristics with our opposite-sex parent. Whether we marry, date, or feel attracted to someone, the resemblance to the parent figure is often striking. Romantic relationships, in a way, provide us with an opportunity to resolve unresolved childhood issues with our parents. Falling in love can sometimes be an unconscious attempt to heal or rewrite the emotional narratives formed in childhood.

The influence of parental images on romantic choice is profound. Our early bonds with caregivers not only shape our ability to form attachments but also lay the groundwork for the romantic relationships we seek in adulthood. Understanding these patterns allows us to gain insight into our choices and the dynamics of our love lives, and may help us address unresolved issues that influence our romantic connections.

Positive Sexual Imprinting

Positive sexual imprinting refers to the phenomenon where individuals seek romantic partners who resemble their opposite-sex parents, both in physical and psychological traits. People who had healthy relationships with their parents—especially with their opposite-sex parent—are more likely to establish romantic connections with individuals who mirror these traits. This can include similarities in facial features, body types, and personality. For instance, as professor Bereczkei noted in a *Telegraph* interview, this pattern can help explain why certain public figures are drawn to partners who resemble their parents. Examples include Kim Wilde's attraction to her husband Hal Fowler, who shares similar features with her father, Marti Wilde, or how Catherine Zeta-Jones' husband, Michael Douglas, shares chin dimples with her father, Dai Jones (Harding, 2004).

Does this idea resonate with you? Do you notice any similarities between your romantic partner and your opposite-sex parent?

The nature of our relationship with our opposite-sex parent has a profound effect on the kind of romantic relationships we develop. For example, a man who had a peaceful and nurturing relationship with his mother might be drawn to a woman who resembles her in both physical appearance and emotional traits. The same holds true for women: a positive relationship with their father may lead them to seek a partner who shares similar traits. The key word here is "serene," describing a relationship without overt or unresolved conflicts.

Psychological conflicts, whether conscious or unconscious, shape the way we interact with others. Conscious conflicts are those we are aware of, while unconscious conflicts are hidden deep within our psyche, often due to their painful nature. When someone is attracted to a partner who resembles their opposite-sex parent, it often signifies a harmonious relationship with that parent, free from deep emotional or psychological conflict.

Individuals who hold no grudges against their opposite-sex parent may internalize their parent's traits as a blueprint for choosing romantic partners. It's not uncommon to observe couples where the daughter's husband resembles her father or the son's wife shares characteristics with his mother. We often look for a partner who provides the security, love, and care we experienced in our early years, particularly if we were raised in a nurturing and conflict-free environment with our opposite-sex parent.

Many people unknowingly model themselves after their same-sex parent, repeating emotional, behavioral, and cognitive patterns in their intimate relationships. This pattern extends to both positive and negative sexual imprinting. In the case of positive sexual imprinting, a romantic partner will often treat an individual in the same way their opposite-sex parent treated their same-sex parent. The relationship dynamics observed in childhood, especially between the opposite-sex parents, serve as a template for future relationships.

For example, if your parents were both kind and caring individuals, you're likely to be attracted to people who show similar levels of compassion and care. A visit to your partner's family can often shed light on why they act the way they do and why they may expect certain behaviors from you. You might notice familiar behavioral patterns that are characteristic of your partner's family dynamics—patterns which are likely to have been communicated through generations and may influence your partner's actions in their relationships.

Before embarking on a serious relationship, it's beneficial to explore your partner's perceptions of their opposite-sex parent and examine the dynamics of their relationship. Gaining insight into how they view and relate to their opposite-sex parent can provide valuable information about their emotional makeup and help identify potential issues that may affect your relationship.

For example, a man who disrespects his mother may struggle to respect women in general. If his mother was unfaithful or unreliable, he may project those same fears and insecurities onto his romantic partner. In contrast, a woman who has unresolved issues with her father might find it difficult to respect men, no matter how kind or caring they are. Such unresolved feelings can manifest in how they treat their partner and affect the relationship's overall health.

Understanding these patterns of behavior is crucial for building a lasting and healthy relationship. By recognizing the influence of family dynamics, you can navigate potential challenges and foster a deeper connection with your partner. Uncovering unresolved family issues can serve as a guide for how to approach and manage your own relationship with greater awareness and sensitivity.

We all come from unique family environments, each with its own set of behaviors and communication patterns. These early experiences shape how we view ourselves and how we engage in relationships. The way we enter into romantic relationships is influenced by the dynamics we were exposed to growing up. The values, beliefs, and behavioral patterns modeled by our parents or caregivers influence how we form and maintain intimate connections.

Ultimately, recognizing that everyone carries some form of emotional baggage from their family background allows us to approach relationships with greater empathy and understanding. By acknowledging these influences, we can work through past issues, embrace personal growth, and develop healthier, more fulfilling relationships.

Negative Sexual Imprinting

Negative sexual imprinting is another significant psychological factor, one that is non-inherited but deeply influences mate preferences. This phenomenon involves an internalized aversion to individuals whose traits resemble those of the opposite-sex parent. For those who did not have a positive relationship with their opposite-sex parent, they are likely to feel repulsed by individuals who share physical or behavioral traits with that parent (Fleming et al., 2002). For instance, physical features that remind them of that parent may immediately turn them off.

Consider a woman who was rejected by her father during childhood. She may unconsciously try to avoid reliving that traumatic experience, which left a profound mark on her psyche. Any man who looks, speaks, or acts like her father may feel like a threat to her emotional well-being, bringing buried feelings of rejection back to the surface. Being with such a man would constantly trigger the fear of being rejected by someone she loves and wants to be with.

Take, for example, a highly successful and attractive woman in her twenties, seemingly having it all—except for a serious romantic relationship. When asked about her love life, she insists that she is too busy to settle down with a man. However, those who know her well understand that this isn't entirely true. She often expresses dissatisfaction about not having a partner. Her professional success has not prevented her from desiring a fulfilling relationship, but there's a deeper issue at play. Despite having suitable dating prospects, she struggles to connect with them. This behavior can be explained by the unconscious feelings common among women who did not have a good relationship with their fathers.

Her career and busy lifestyle are not the main obstacles. Rather, she may unconsciously avoid men who remind her of her father. This protective instinct, developed during her childhood, stems from witnessing her father, a successful business consultant, abandon her mother for another woman. As a young child, she observed the immense pain her mother endured after being left behind. To avoid repeating this pain, she has unconsciously steered clear of successful men who bear similarities to her father.

Negative sexual imprinting suggests that unresolved, painful feelings buried in the unconscious play a crucial role in our mate choices. The fear of selecting a partner who mirrors the traits of a parent with whom we had negative emotional experiences influences the decisions we make in love. Our social history and past emotional wounds often dictate the types of partners we choose (Lammers, 2011).

Have you ever wondered why someone might avoid dating a man who has his life together? Could he remind her of her father? The woman mentioned earlier may offer some clarity. Her father's departure left her with a deep fear of abandonment, which she subconsciously seeks to avoid. This avoidance strategy explains why she may find herself steering clear of men who resemble her father's successful, emotionally distant persona.

When it comes to romantic attraction, a "protective attitude" is an unconscious defense mechanism against replicating past relationship patterns or enduring painful emotional experiences (Beck, 1976). While this attitude may seem protective, it can have disastrous effects on one's romantic life, leading to destructive dating habits and relationship dynamics. Often, individuals with this mindset aren't aware of the psychological reasons behind their behavior, which makes it difficult for them to articulate the true cause of their actions. For example, someone who frequently sabotages their relationships might rationalize their behavior, but this is driven by a deep fear of rejection.

Many people unknowingly repeat the same patterns across different relationships. This unconscious desire to protect themselves from perceived emotional pain leads to predictable outcomes in their love lives. Those who engage in such patterns need to recognize that these recurring issues will only lay the foundation for a cycle of unsuccessful relationships. Awareness of their parents' emotional dynamics can help break this destructive cycle and lead to healthier relationship choices.

What's particularly intriguing about negative sexual imprinting is that, despite consciously trying to avoid certain traits or relationship patterns, individuals often end up attracted to the very qualities they seek to avoid. If you reflect on your dating history, you might notice that you've often been drawn to people who exhibit traits you dislike. The very behaviors you hoped to avoid resurface in your relationships, often due to the unresolved emotional patterns from your past.

These patterns become evident when a person's behavior shifts after the initial stages of a relationship. In the beginning, someone may appear to act in a certain way, but once a deeper connection forms, the behavior changes. Why does this happen? The truth is, these individuals don't change; they simply reveal sides of themselves that were hidden at first. The unresolved conflicts from their past, as well as the dynamics of the relationship, trigger these behaviors.

It's a well-known psychological fact that the environment and interactions with others can influence one's behavior. People often act differently depending on who they're interacting with. In romantic relationships, unhealthy adjustments are sometimes made to accommodate unresolved emotional conflicts from the past. For example, if you are in a relationship with someone who has low self-esteem, you may find yourself taking on a role that caters to their emotional needs. But for this dynamic to work, you must also have low self-esteem.

Low self-esteem couples tend to nurture each other's idealized self-image, and this relationship is characterized by a constant give-and-take. The person boosting their partner's ego also derives narcissistic benefits, which can create a vicious cycle. When someone lacks self-confidence, they may unconsciously seek a partner who can help them escape from their true self and instead attach to an idealized version of themselves.

In the end, negative sexual imprinting often leads us to seek partners who reflect the unresolved conflicts of our past. Understanding these patterns can help break the cycle and lead to healthier relationships, allowing individuals to address their fears of abandonment and self-worth in a more constructive manner.

Human Sexuality

Human sexuality is a deeply rooted and multifaceted aspect of our lives that influences identity, relationships, and personal fulfillment. It goes far beyond biology—encompassing emotion, culture, psychology, and individual values. Understanding sexuality means recognizing its complexity, its dynamic nature, and the powerful role it plays both in shaping individuals and influencing society at large.

One of the most compelling features of human sexuality is its diversity. Throughout history, various cultures and institutions have tried to define or control sexual behavior through laws, traditions, and moral codes. Yet in today's world, we are increasingly aware that sexuality is fluid, personal, and not easily confined to rigid labels. The growing acceptance of varied sexual orientations, gender identities, and relationship structures reflects a more nuanced understanding of what it means to be human. This evolving perspective challenges outdated norms and encourages inclusivity and empathy.

Sexuality is also central to how we connect with others. Feelings of love, attraction, and intimacy are essential to emotional health and relational satisfaction. Open, honest conversations about sex and consent have become crucial for nurturing respectful, meaningful relationships. Comprehensive sex education and dialogue help to break down harmful myths, reduce stigma, and empower individuals to make informed, confident decisions about their bodies and relationships.

Despite this progress, many still face significant challenges related to sexuality. Social pressures, cultural taboos, discrimination, and unrealistic portrayals in the media can contribute to feelings of shame, confusion, or inadequacy. The intersection of sexuality with issues like gender norms, religious beliefs, and political agendas often gives rise to contentious debates about rights, autonomy, and moral values.

In essence, human sexuality is a journey of discovery—one that involves growth, learning, and the exploration of self. Through personal experiences, relationships, or scholarly inquiry, engaging with our sexuality allows for deeper self-awareness and empathy toward others. By promoting acceptance, education, and open-mindedness, we can foster a society in which everyone feels safe and respected in expressing their authentic selves without fear or shame.

The Multidisciplinary Approach to Human Sexuality

Understanding human sexuality requires a comprehensive, multidisciplinary approach that integrates biological, psychological, social, and cultural perspectives. Sexuality is not shaped by a single factor but is instead a complex interplay of systems that influence behavior, identity, and expression.

Biologically, human sexuality is rooted in genetics, hormones, and neurological processes. Hormones like testosterone and estrogen play a key role in sexual development, attraction, and behavior (Bancroft, 2009). The brain is central to sexual functioning, with regions such as the hypothalamus and the limbic system governing sexual arousal and desire (LeVay, 2011).

From a psychological standpoint, sexuality is influenced by thoughts, emotions, developmental experiences, and learned behaviors. Sigmund Freud's theory of psychosexual development emphasized the impact of early childhood experiences on adult sexual identity (Freud, 1905). Modern perspectives, such as Bandura's social learning theory, argue that sexual attitudes and behaviors are shaped through observation, imitation, and reinforcement within one's environment (Bandura, 1977).

Social and cultural factors further shape how sexuality is understood and expressed. Cultural norms, religious doctrines, and societal values create frameworks that define what is considered acceptable or taboo. Philosopher Michel Foucault (1978) argued that sexuality is a social construct, influenced by historical and political power structures. Additionally, concepts like gender roles and sexual scripts—culturally defined expectations of how individuals should behave sexually—guide individual sexual expression (Gagnon & Simon, 1973).

Sexual orientation, or the enduring pattern of romantic or sexual attraction toward others, is also a key component of human sexuality. Alfred Kinsey and colleagues introduced the Kinsey Scale (1948), which proposed a spectrum of sexual orientation rather than a strict heterosexual-homosexual binary. Today's research supports a more nuanced understanding, recognizing that both biological predispositions and environmental influences contribute to sexual orientation (Bailey et al., 2016).

In sum, human sexuality is a deeply integrated aspect of life that cannot be fully understood through a single lens. By drawing on biological, psychological, and sociocultural perspectives, we gain a richer, more holistic understanding of how sexuality develops, is experienced, and varies across individuals and societies.

Lovemaking

When we speak about love and romantic relationships, the topic of lovemaking must naturally follow. Sexuality is a profound expression of the self — the way we experience and express ourselves as sexual beings mirrors our deepest emotional truths. During sexual intimacy, the barriers we often maintain in everyday life begin to dissolve. Our fears, desires, vulnerabilities, and instincts come forward. This is the moment when the "persona" — the socially constructed mask we present to the world — is stripped away, quite literally and metaphorically.

It's no coincidence that sex involves physical nakedness; it is perhaps one of the few areas in life where authenticity becomes nearly impossible to fake. Of course, people may pretend to enjoy the act or even fake orgasm, but the body itself — governed by the autonomic nervous system — reveals deeper truths. Unlike the voluntary nervous system that controls walking or speaking, the autonomic system oversees involuntary functions like increased heart rate and heavy breathing, which often accompany sexual arousal. These responses are not easily manipulated by conscious will, making sex one of the most revealing human experiences.

Human sexuality has existed as long as humanity itself. Throughout history, sex has been pursued not only for reproduction but also for pleasure, emotional connection, and intimacy. While procreation is one biological function of sex, many people engage in it far more often for enjoyment and bonding. Across time and cultures, questions of how to give and receive pleasure have driven curiosity and exploration. Texts like the *Kama Sutra* — written between 400 BCE and 200 CE — serve as ancient testimonies to our long-standing desire to refine and understand the art of lovemaking.

When we strip away societal pretense, many would agree that poor sexual compatibility can weaken a relationship. A fulfilling sex life often strengthens emotional bonds, deepens trust, and enhances communication. In many ways, sexual intimacy represents the ultimate level of emotional and physical closeness between two people. Consider the simple but symbolic nature of romantic acts: holding hands, kissing, or intercourse. Each represents a form of mutual giving — an offering of oneself. Kissing is not merely a brush of lips; it's an exchange of intimacy. Intercourse, at its most meaningful, is an act of complete connection.

Because our sexual expression is so closely tied to our inner world, changes in our sex life often require deep internal reflection. Quick fixes like Viagra or Cialis may offer temporary physical solutions, but they cannot resolve the underlying psychological or emotional issues. A man struggling with erectile dysfunction rooted in low self-esteem or fear of inadequacy may find only limited relief through medication if the deeper cause remains unaddressed. Similarly, a woman who has endured trauma may struggle with trust and physical openness in intimate encounters, not because of physical dysfunction but because of emotional scars.

Sexual issues often originate not in the body, but in the psyche — in the irrational, unconscious part of the mind. In a sexual context, this part of the mind becomes the "playing field" where internal conflicts silently compete. One might feel like a bystander, watching a game unfold that is beyond conscious control. A man does not will an erection into existence; his mind permits or withholds it, based on internal beliefs and emotional comfort. The bedroom, then, is not the battlefield to resolve psychological wounds — the mind is. Attempting to fix performance issues solely in bed is like trying to fight a war with no enemy in sight; the true opponent lies within.

Ultimately, to improve our sex lives, we must confront the fears, traumas, and insecurities that influence our intimate experiences. Healing begins with awareness. If the mind is holding you back, it's the mind that must be explored and nurtured. Only then can lovemaking evolve from a physical act to a deeply transformative connection — a reflection of who you are, and how much of yourself you're truly willing to share.

Conclusion

Romantic choices often feel intensely personal, yet they are influenced by a complex interplay of subconscious patterns, emotional histories, societal conditioning, and unmet psychological needs. As we reflect on our relationships, recurring patterns — both constructive and destructive — may become apparent, prompting us to ask: *Why am I drawn to certain people?* and *What do these choices reveal about me?*

One of the most profound insights about romantic attraction is that it often mirrors our internal emotional world. Our attachment styles, usually shaped by early life experiences, play a central role in how we seek connection and intimacy. Some individuals yearn for closeness and emotional safety, while others unconsciously gravitate toward emotionally distant partners in an attempt to heal unresolved childhood wounds. Recognizing these patterns is the first step toward forming healthier, more fulfilling relationships.

Cultural influences also shape our romantic ideals. Family expectations, media portrayals, and societal narratives frequently inform our beliefs about who we should love. These external forces can subtly lead us to pursue partners who fit a socially acceptable mold, rather than those who align with our authentic needs. Unpacking these layers of influence helps us make romantic choices that are grounded in self-awareness, rather than cultural conformity.

Timing and life circumstances are also critical. Who we are drawn to at one stage of life may not align with who we become later. Personal growth reshapes our values, goals, and emotional needs, often requiring a reevaluation of our romantic decisions. Embracing this evolution instead of resisting it opens the door to relationships that reflect who we are today — not who we once were.

Gaining insight into our romantic behavior is not about self-blame, but about cultivating self-awareness. Without this awareness, we risk reliving the same painful cycles — rejection, abandonment, or emotional neglect — over and over. In our effort to avoid these hurts, we often develop protective mechanisms that ultimately sabotage connection. Each new relationship becomes an opportunity not for healing, but for reenacting old emotional scripts, unless we consciously intervene.

Denial is another powerful obstacle to healthy love. Many people find it easier to blame their partners than to acknowledge their own role in relationship struggles. We often consume self-help content or relationship advice with others in mind, rather than reflecting on our own behavior. This deflection blinds us to the changes we need to make within ourselves, reinforcing destructive patterns.

Romantic attraction isn't solely rational — nor should it be. While thoughtful decision-making plays a role, unconscious drives rooted in our emotional and psychological makeup have a powerful influence. Relationally dependent individuals may feel compelled to be in a relationship at any cost, using love as a source of validation. In contrast, relationally independent individuals often approach love with a focus on character and compatibility, seeking partners whose values resonate with their own.

To remove the unconscious from the equation of love is to strip romance of its passion and mystery. The intense emotions love inspires often stem from the unconscious — that part of ourselves beyond reason or logic. Passionate love is inherently irrational and instinctive. It doesn't stem from careful analysis but from a deep emotional resonance that defies intellectual explanation. This type of love, unlike familial or "filial" love, is fueled by desire and emotional vulnerability.

Nonetheless, lasting romantic relationships require more than passion. True intimacy comes from understanding the hidden motives behind our attraction and behavior. Without this awareness, we risk sabotaging even the most promising connections. The key lies in exploring not just *who* we are attracted to, but *why* — a journey that often leads us to discover unconscious fears, unmet needs, and unhealed wounds.

Romantic relationships, when approached with self-awareness, are powerful arenas for personal transformation. Love has a unique ability to illuminate the parts of ourselves that need healing and growth. It invites us to examine our beliefs, values, and emotional patterns — and in doing so, it expands our capacity for connection, empathy, and personal evolution.

Ultimately, the more conscious we become of our motivations in love, the more empowered we are to break free from destructive cycles and build relationships that truly nourish and support us. Love, then, becomes not just a feeling, but a conscious path toward wholeness.

References

American Psychiatric Association. (2013). *Diagnostic and Statistical Manual of Mental Disorders (5th ed.)*. Washington, DC: APA.

Aron, A., & Aron, E. N. (1986). *Love and the expansion of self: Understanding attraction and s satisfaction. Advances in Experimental Social P Psychology*, 19, 1-52.

Aron, A., Fisher, H., Mashek, D. J., Strong, G., Li, H., Brown, L. L. (2005). Reward, motivation, and emotion systems associated with early-stage Intense romantic love. *Journal of Neurophysiology, 94*(1), 327-337.

Bailey, J. M., Dunne, M. P., & Martin, N. G. (2016). Genetic and Environmental Influences on Sexual Psychological Science in the Public Interest, 17(2), 45–70.

Bancroft, J. (2009). *Human Sexuality and Its Problems*. Elsevier.

Bandura, A. (1977). Social Learning Theory. Prentice-Hall.

Bartholomew, K., & Horowitz, L. M. (1991). Attachment styles among young adults: A test of four-category model. *Journal of Personality and Social Psychology, 61*(2), 226-244.

Beck, A. T. (1976). *Cognitive Therapy and the Emotional Disorders*. International Universities Press.

Bereczkei, T. (2009). Facialmetric similarities mediate mate choice: Sexual imprinting on opposite-sex parents. Proceedings of the Royal Society,276 (1654), 91-98. DOI: 10.1098/rspb. 20 08.1021.

Bowlby, J. (1969). *Attachment and Loss:Vol.1. Attachment*. New York: Basic Books.

Brand, R. J., Bonatsos, A., D'Orazio, R., DeShong, H. (2012). What is beautiful is good, even online: Correlation between photo attractiveness and text attractiveness in men's online dating profiles, Villanova University, Computer in Human Behavior, Volume 28, Issue 1, pg. 166-170 http//dx.doi.org/10. 1016/j.chb .2011.08.023.

Brunell, A. B., & Campbell, W. K. (2011). Narcissism and romantic relationships: Understanding the paradox. *The Handbook of Narcissism and Narcissistic Personality Disorder*, 344-350.

Buss, D. M. (1989). *Sex differences in human mate preferences: Evolutionary hypotheses tested in 3 37 cultures.* Behavioral and Brain Sciences, 12(1), 149.

Buss, D. M., & Schmitt, D. P. (1993). *Sexual strategies theory: An evolutionary perspective on human mating.* Psychological Review, 100(2), 204-232.

Campbell, W. K., & Foster, J. D. (2007). The narcissistic self: Background, an extended agency model, and ongoing controversies. *Frontiers in Psychology, 3*(2), 1-11.

Carroll, L. (1865). *Alice's Adventures in Wonderland.* Macmillan.

Carson, R. C. (1969). *Interaction concepts of personality.* Chicago: Aldine. Dowling, C. (1982). Women's Hidden Fear of Independence. Pocket Book

Cohen, S., & Wills, T. A. (1985). *Stress, social support, and the buffering hypothesis. Psychological Bulletin*, 98(2), 310-357.

Dennis, H. (2009). Learning by Imprinting: Understanding Behavior Based on Phase-Sensitive Learning, Science and literature, http://www .suite101.com/content/learning-by-imprinting -a136714).

Diamond, L. M. (2003). What does sexual orientation orient? A biobehavioral model distinguishing romantic love and sexual desire. *Psychological Review, 110*(1), 173–192.

Dickinson, K. A., & Pincus, A. L. (2003). Interpersonal analysis of grandiose and vulnerable narcissism. *Journal of Personality Disorders, 17*(3), 188-207.

Dixson, B. J., & Brooks, R. C. (2013). *Facial masculinity and health in men: Effects of testosterone and immune system functioning.* Evolutionary Psychology, 11(3), 450-466.

Dowling, C. (1981). The Cinderella Complex: Women's Hidden Fear of Independence. Summit Books.

Dryer, D., Christopher, H., Leonard, M. (1997). When do opposites attract? Interpersonal complementarity versus similarity, Journal of Personality and Social Psychology, Vol 72(3), pg. 592-603.

Dutton, D. G., & Painter, S. L. (1981). *Traumatic bonding: The development of emotional attachments in battered women and other relationships of intermittent abuse. Victimology,* 6(1), 139-155.

Estrade, P. (1991). Le Couple Retrouvé. Editions Dangles

Eastwick, P. W., Finkel, E. J., & Eagly, A. H. (2012). When and why do ideal partner preferences affect the process of initiating and maintaining romantic relationships? *Journal of Personality and Social Psychology,* 103(5), 862-888.

Fisher, H. (2004). *Why We Love: The Nature and Chemistry of Romantic Love.* Henry Holt and Company.

Fisher, H. E., Brown, L. L., Aron, A., Strong, G., &
Mashek, D. (2010). Reward, addiction, and
emotion regulation systems associated with
rejection in love. *Journal of Neurophysiology,
104*(1), 51-60.

Fleming, A. S., Corter, C., Stallings, J., & Friesen, W.
(2002). The role of early experience in the
development of sexual preferences. *Archives of
Sexual Behavior, 31*(1), 43-60. [DOI: 10.1023
/A:1015034103675]

Foster, J. D., Shrira, I., & Campbell, W. K. (2003).
Theoretical models of narcissism, relationship
commitment, and relationship functioning. *In W.
K. Campbell & R. M. Miller (Eds.), The Handbook
of Narcissism and Narcissistic Personality
Disorder* (pp. 193-205). Wiley.

Foucault, M. (1978). The History of Sexuality: Volume
1. Pantheon Books.

Frager, R., & Fadiman, J. (2005). Personality and
Personal Growth (6th ed.). Pearson Prentice Hall
pg.56.

Franck, T. (2005). Love as Mental Illness: Love Sick,
Thunder's Mouth Press.

Freud, S. (1920). *Beyond the Pleasure Principle*.
Norton.

Freud, S. (1927). *The Ego and the Id.* Hogarth Press.

Freud, S. (1914/1957). *On Narcissism: An
Introduction.* Standard Edition, Vol. 14. Hogarth
Press.

Freud, S. (1905/1953). *Three Essays on the Theory of
Sexuality.* Standard Edition, Vol. 7. Hogarth
Press.

Freud, S. (1910/1957). *A Special Type of Choice of
Object Made by Men.* Standard Edition, Vol. 11.
Hogarth Press.

Gagnon, J. H., & Simon, W. (1973). *Sexual Conduct:
The Social Sources of Human Sexuality.* Aldine.

Grammer, K., Fink, B., & Neave, N. (2005). Human
pheromones and sexual attraction. *European
Journal of Obstetrics & Gynecology and
Reproductive Biology, 118*(2), 135-142.

Geher, G. (2000). Perceived and actual characteristics of parents and partners: A test of a Freudian model of mate selection. Current Psychology, 19 (3), 194-214, DOI: 10.1007/s12144-000-1015-7.

Griffiths, R., & Dutton, E. (2011). *Beauty and symmetry: Evolutionary explanations of Preferences for attractiveness*. Journal of Evolutionary Psychology, 9(4), 233-249.

Harding, T. (2004). *Men and women choose partners who look like their parents, study suggests*. The Telegraph. Retrieved from www.telegraph.co.uk

Hazan, C., & Shaver, P. R. (1987). *Romantic love conceptualized as an attachment process. J Journal of Personality and Social Psychology*, 52(3), 511- 524.

Hendrick, C., & Hendrick, S. S. (1992). Romantic love. *Sage Series on Close Relationships.*

Hess, E. H. (1958). *Imprinting in animals*. Scientific American, 198(6), 81-90.

Highfield, R. (2008). Children use opposite sex parent as template for a partner, https://www.

telegraph.co.uk/news/science/science-news/
3350942.

Jonason, P. K., et al. (2013). *The role of narcissism in predicting attraction to dark triad traits. Personality and Individual Differences*, 55(2), 143-148.

Jennifer S. D. (2004). Eeffects of heritable mating preferences, Rochester Institute of Technology.

Jung, C. G. (1953). *Two Essays on Analytical Psychology*. Princeton University Press.

Jung, C. G. (1959). *Aion: Researches into the Phenomenology of the Self*. Princeton University Press.

Jung, C. G. (1953). *Psychological Aspects of the Self. Collected Works*, Vol. 9, Part 1. Princeton University Press.

Jung, C. G. (1969). *The Archetypes and the Collective Unconscious*. Princeton University Press.

Kelley, H. H., & Thibaut, J. W. (1978). *Interpersonal relationships: A theory of interdependence*. Wiley-Interscience.

Kernberg, O. (1975). *Borderline Conditions and Pathological Narcissism.* New York: Jason Aronson.

Kinsey, A. C., Pomeroy, W. B., & Martin, C. E. (1948). *Sexual Behavior in the Human Male.* W.B. Saunders.

Kohut, H. (1971). *The Analysis of the Self: A Systematic Approach to the Psychoanalytic Treatment of   Narcissistic Personality Disorders.* International   Universities Press.

Lammers, J., Stoker, J. I., Jordan, J., Pollmann, M., & Fischer, A. H. (2011). Power Increases Infidelity: Exploring the Link Between Power and Misbehavior. *Psychological Science, 22*(9), 1197–1202. DOI: 10.1177/0956797611416252.

LeVay, S. (2011). *Gay, Straight, and the Reason Why: Yhe Science of Sexual Orientation.* Oxford University Press.

Little, A. C., Penton-Voak, I. S., Burt, D. M., & Perrett, D. I. (2003). A test of a Freudian model of mate choice: Transference effects in preferences for opposite-sex faces. *Proceedings of the Royal Society of London. Series B: Biological Sciences, 270*(1526), 2283-2288. https://doi.org/10.1098 rspb.2003.2505

Lorenz, K. (1935). *Der Kumpan in der Umwelt des Vogels*. Journal für Ornithologie, 83(3), 137– 213.

Markus J. Rantala, M, Urszula, M. (2010). The role of sexual imprinting and the Westermarck effect in mate choice in humans, Behav Ecol Sociobiol DOI 10.1007/s00265-011-1145-y.

Marazziti, D., Akiskal, H. S., Rossi, A., & Cassano, G. B. (1999). Alteration of the platelet serotonin transporter in romantic love. *Psychological Medicine, 29*(3), 741-745.

Mikulincer, M., & Shaver, P. R. (2007). *Attachment in adulthood: Structure, dynamics, and change. Guilford Press.*

Miller, J. D., Lynam, D. R., Hyatt, C. S., & Campbell, W. K. (2017). Controversies in narcissism. *Annual Review of Clinical Psychology, 13*(1), 291-315.

https://doi.org/10.1146/annurev-clinpsy-032816-045244

Murray, S. L., Holmes, J. G., & Griffin, D. W. (1996). *The Self-Fulfilling Nature of Positive Illusions in Romantic Relationships.* Journal of Personality and Social Psychology, 71(6), 1155–180.

Penton-Voak, I. S., et al. (1999). *Female preference for male faces changes cyclically: Further evidence of hormonal influences.* Behavioral Ecology and Sociobiology, 45(1), 1-12.

Plato. *Symposium.* Translated by Benjamin Jowett, 1892.

Plato. *Symposium*, 178a–222b. In *The Complete Works of Plato*, edited by John M. Cooper, Hackett Publishing, 1997.

Rhodes, G. (2006). *The evolutionary psychology of facial attractiveness.* Annual Review of Psychology, 57, 199-226.

Schaal, B., et al. (1997). *Major histocompatibility complex and mate selection: A functional perspective. Journal of Evolutionary Biology,* 10(1), 55-66.

Tennov, D. (1979). *Love and Limerence: The Experience of Being in Love.* Scarborough House.

Trivers, R. (1972). *Parental investment and sexual selection.* In B. Campbell (Ed.), *Sexual Selection and the Descent of Man* (pp. 136-179). Aldine.

Winch, R. F. (1958). *Mate selection: A study of complementary needs. The Journal of Social Psychology,* 48(1), 51-56.

Watson, P. J., Grisham, S. O., Trotter, M. V., Biderman, M. D. (1984). Narcissism and empathy: Validity evidence for the Narcissistic Personality Inventory. *Journal of Personality Assessment, 48*(3),301-305. https://doi.org/10. 1207/s153 27752jpa 4803_12.

Young, L. J., & Wang, Z. (2004). The neurobiology of Pair bonding. *Nature Neuroscience, 7*(10), 1048-1054.